PRIMEVAL MAN

See Page 102.

PRIMEVAL MAN

An Examination of some Recent Speculations

BY THE DUKE OF ARGYLL

NEW YORK:
DE WITT C. LENT & CO.
451 BROOME STREET
1872

PREFACE.

HAVING now no immediate prospect of being able to expand or to illustrate the argument contained in the following pages, I republish it with very little alteration from the form in which it originally appeared in "Good Words." I am well aware how much it requires both expansion and illustration. But I hope that at least the main lines of that argument are traced with sufficient clearness to enable others with more leisure to pursue them farther, and to test the results arrived at by our growing knowledge in the sciences which bear upon the early condition of Mankind. The distinctions here taken between different branches of the subject, have not, so far as I know, been elsewhere laid down with adequate precision. Yet all safe reasoning depends upon such distinctions being carefully observed. If they are sound, they place an insuperable bar in the way of certain conclusions respecting Primeval Man, which have been too hastily assumed as following from recently discovered facts. At all events these conclusions can only be reached by new arguments and by new methods of proof.

Many of the questions which are involved in the reasoning of this Essay, are questions which touch upon the profoundest problems of our nature and of our history:—On the connection, seemingly inseparable, between all mental phenomena and physical organization; on the truthfulness of any system of classification which does not take equal cognizance of both; on the distinction between intellectual powers and moral character; on the distinction, again, between the mere results of accumulated knowledge, and the working of the original faculties of Reason; on the question how far the first use and the first direction of his mental powers may have been as purely instinctive in Man as in the Bee or in the Beaver; on the relation between the two tendencies in Man to advance and to decline; on the causes of degradation which are born with him and seem to be inseparable from his nature; on the bearing upon the whole argument of existing facts respecting his distribution on the globe, and the obvious effects upon him of hardship and of suffering to produce, or to intensify, a barbarous condition;—on each and all of these questions, which enter into the reasoning of this Essay, whole volumes might be written without exhausting what is to be said upon them. I shall be content, in the meantime, if this slight sketch of so great a subject should be of any use in directing others into some well-defined paths of thought and of investigation in regard to it.

LONDON, *Dec.* 9, 1868.

CONTENTS.

PART I.

INTRODUCTORY.

AT the meeting, in 1867, of the British Association for the Advancement of Science, a paper was read by Sir J. Lubbock upon "The Early Condition of Mankind." It purports to be a reply to a lecture on the "Origin of Civilization" by Dr. Whately, the late Archbishop of Dublin, which was published in 1854. The Archbishop's position is shortly this,—that mere savages—that is to say, "men in the lowest degree, or even anything approaching to the lowest degree, of barbarism in which they can possibly subsist at all—never did and never can, unaided, raise themselves into a higher condition;" that even when they are brought into contact with superior races, it is extremely difficult to teach them the simplest arts; that they "seem never to invent or discover anything," because even "necessity is not the mother of invention except to those who have some degree of thoughtfulness and intelligence;" that whatever the natural powers of the human mind may be, they require to have some instruction from without wherewith to start. He holds it to be "a complete moral certainty that men left unassisted in what is called a state of nature—that is, with the faculties Man is born with not at all unfolded or exercised by education—never did, and never can, raise themselves from that condition." Therefore, "according to the present course of things, the first introducer of civilization among savages is, and must be, man in a more improved state." But as "in the beginning of the human race there was no *man* to effect it," this must have been the work of another Being. "There must have been, in short, something of a revelation made to the first or to some subsequent generation of our species." The conclusion is that, as Man must have had a Divine Creator, it seems equally certain that, to some extent also, he must have had a Divine Instructor.

This is the argument which Sir J. Lubbock

has undertaken to refute. His conclusion is, that the "primitive condition of mankind was one of utter barbarism;" that from this condition certain races have independently raised themselves; and, of course, that, instead of existing savages being the degenerate descendants of ancestors who were more advanced, all races now civilized are the children of men who were once in the same low condition. A further conclusion, though not formally asserted, is plainly indicated, viz. this, —that the "utter barbarism" of the first man was itself an advance on the condition of some progenitor. I infer that this idea is intended to be conveyed when the "first men" are explained to mean the "first beings worthy to be so called."

The two main lines of argument pursued by Sir J. Lubbock connect themselves with the two following propositions which he undertakes to prove:—1st, "That there are indications of progress even among savages;" and 2d, "That among the most civilized nations there are traces of original barbarism."

Sir J. Lubbock's paper has confirmed an impression I have long had, that Whately's argument, though strong at some points, is at others open to assault; and that, as a whole, the subject now requires to be differently handled, and regarded from a different point of view. On the other hand, the same paper has convinced me that the argument in favour of what may be called the Savage-theory is very much the weaker of the two, and rests upon a method of treatment much more inadequate and incomplete.

I propose in this, and in some following chapters, to set forth the reasoning upon which these convictions rest.

There are, however, some preliminary considerations which it may be well to deal with before proceeding farther.

It will be observed that both arguments are avowedly conducted irrespective of any belief in the Mosaic narrative of Creation. They both profess to be purely scientific; that is, founded on natural knowledge, and using for the discovery of truth such facts and inferences as are ascertainable by reason. Whately expressly says that in his argument he has not appealed to the Book of Genesis as an authority, because he "thought it important to show, independently of that authority and from a monument actually before our eyes—the existence, namely, of civilized man—that there is no escaping such conclusions as agree with the Bible narrative." The opposite argument is, of course, maintained always from the same basis of scientific independence, and those who urge it do not generally profess or care to reconcile the conclusion arrived at, with the Mosaic narrative. Sir J. Lubbock at the close of his paper says emphatically, "These views follow, I think, from strictly scientific considerations." No doubt, if the inquiry is to be pursued at all upon this basis, it must be conducted honestly, and the conclusions legitimately reached must be accepted with just so much of conviction as is justified by the nature of the data, and the nature of the reasoning employed.

The question may well arise in many minds in reference to this subject, whether it is a legitimate subject of speculation at all—whether it does not transcend our faculties to ascertain the truth.

Respecting this question, there is one answer which is obvious, although it may not go far to satisfy those whose scruples are most sincere. When men in the position of the late Archbishop of Dublin enter upon this discussion, and declare that, independent of all authority, certain conclusions can be shown to be unavoidable by natural reason, we cannot prohibit others from entering upon the same ground, or from producing such arguments as they may be able to find in support of an opposite conclusion. But there are some better arguments than this. This, indeed, is enough to show that the discussion must, as a matter of necessity, be encountered, even though it should be deplored. But other considerations may perhaps convince us that it ought not to be avoided. It may be true, and I believe it to be true, that the desire of knowledge is capable of excess. The spirit which in the ordinary concerns of life is condemned as idle or vicious curiosity has, surely, its counterpart in the higher pursuits of intellect. David seems to imply as much when he pleads in favour of his own character and conduct before God—"I do not exercise myself in things too high for me." On the other hand, we must remember that in nothing has the human race been more liable to the delusions of superstition than in the conception of the matters which were to be held, or were not to be held, as forbidden to investigation. Those physical laws of nature which are now so familiar to us as the peculiar field of observation and discovery—a field on which the march of intellect has been so rapid and so triumphant—were once held by the early Greek philosophers as belonging to the most secret things of God. They thought, perhaps not unnaturally, that a region which lay, or seemed to lie, so much nearer to themselves, even their own mind and spirit—its phenomena and its methods of procedure—must be the ground most open to their search, and must afford results most comprehensible to the understanding. And so they plunged into all the problems of Metaphysics. But there are no mysteries so deep as these—none in which the human mind reaches so soon the limit of its powers—none in which the temptation is stronger to strain after knowledge which is shrouded in impenetrable darkness. The greatest intellects which the world has ever seen have laboured at such problems, and, in respect at least to many of them, have left them as they found them. The same tendency of metaphysical speculation, blending, through the school of Alexandria, with the mysticism of the East, infected the Theology of the early Church, and heretics were not seldom divided from the orthodox upon questions which were not only beyond the reach of reason, but equally beyond the scope of Revelation. In the Confessions of St. Augustine there is a curious indication of this transposition of the questions which are deemed to be the most legitimate, and the most accessible, subjects of our research. In early life he had been, as is well known, led away by the dangerous speculations which pass in ecclesiastical history under the name of the Manichæan heresy. He pours out his lamentations over the subtleties which had once engrossed and perplexed his mind — subtleties of which

Christianity had revealed the folly. And among the temptations which he still desires to overcome is the appetite of knowledge —a "vain and curious desire hiding under the name of science" (lib. x. c. 35). This is the desire which pretends, he says, to reach the inmost secrets of nature—secrets which when discovered could have no value, and of which men desire and expect nothing except to know. Now, here we have an exact definition of the true scientific spirit —a spirit which has, indeed, in its results, richly "endowed the human family with new mercies," but which never has had this dower in view as its only, or even as its chief, inducement. It is not perhaps exactly relevant to observe that the glorious facts of Astronomy are among the secrets of nature which Augustine rejoices to say he no longer desires to know; because, in his mind, Astronomy took the form of Astrology, to which in his youth he had been much addicted. But Augustine is right when he detects this same love of mere knowledge in the instinctive arrest of his attention by the commonest works of nature. He desires to be delivered even from this. He has given up many pleasures of the eye and curiosities of the mind in which he once delighted,—not only the transits of the heavenly bodies and the response of oracles, but even the public spectacles of the Roman world. Still, he deplores that this wretched love of mere knowledge,—this lust of the eyes,—is ever pursuing him as he walks and lives. Although no longer tempted to go to the Amphitheatre to see the race of hound and hare, he complains that the same sight, if seen accidentally in the fields, will divert his attention from some profound meditation. Even from the windows of his home his eye is caught by some little lizard catching flies upon the wall, or by some spider spreading for the capture her wondrous web. The smallness of these creatures, he confesses, does not diminish his instinctive curiosity. True it is that he might pass from these creatures to magnify the Creator of them all. But he is conscious that this was not present to his thoughts when they were arrested and fixed upon the things he saw.

Most true! and equally true was it that this desire of knowledge was burning intensely in him when it wrung from him no confession; or rather, when it was interwoven into the very tissue of which his immortal Confessions are composed. In them no more splendid passages occur than those in which he turns the eye of his curiosity inwards upon the secrets of his own nature, and asks a thousand unanswerable questions on the structure and the power of Memory. What and where are those innumerable chambers,—those vast halls,—which hold in perpetual imagery not only all he had ever seen, but all he had ever conceived and known? How can the immensities of Time and Space, of earth, and sky, and ocean, be thus contained?

How can they be recalled into what seemed a lost existence? What depths and mysteries of being! How little can we understand ourselves! Does it not seem then as if the mind were too narrow to comprehend itself? And so, through pages of most subtle and eloquent analysis, he revels in that faculty of Wonder, which is the very root and principle of all curious inquiry. I do not say that these questions are wholly vain. But they are useful only as all knowledge may be useful, in teaching us—if it be nothing else—how small that knowledge is. St. Augustine was right in thinking that this wonderful power of Memory lies close to the final secrets on which our very being and personality depend. An eminent philosopher of our own time has found in Memory the only insuperable difficulty in the way of reducing the definition of ourselves into that of mere "Possibilities of Feeling."* But in pursuing these speculations into the most inscrutable of all subjects, St. Augustine is but following the instincts of the same restless and curious intellect which had once struggled with the questions, What Matter is, and How Evil came to be? There is no inquiry in which the human mind comes so immediately to the limit of its powers, as in the analysis of itself. Inscrutable questions may indeed be asked as to what Man once was. But questions much more inscrutable

* Mr. J. S. Mill. I have discussed elsewhere the logic and the adequacy of this definition:—"The Reign of Law." Fifth Edition. Note D.

may be asked, and are habitually asked, as to what Man now is. No conclusions in respect to the original condition of our race can be more shocking to reason and common sense, than many conclusions which metaphysicians have pretended to establish respecting its condition now.

Another reason against declining this inquiry, is to be found in the fact that the plea of impotence against the human understanding, is a plea which may be urged in the service of the most irrational error, as easily as, perhaps more easily than, in the service of the most certain truths. Men engrossed by some particular theory are under immense temptation to denounce the power of faculties whose function it is to apprehend ideas differing from their own. At the present moment this is the habitual practice of a whole school of thinkers, who have eyes for nothing but a particular class of facts, and who therefore very naturally resort to the assertion that all eyes with a wider range of vision are eyes of "phantasy." And if this has been sometimes the result of the anatomy of Mind, what are we to say of the anatomy of the Body? We cannot even think of our bodily frames without encountering at once all the facts which connect the phenomena of Mind with the structure and condition of Material Organs. And then our Organism as a whole, how close it stands to that of the beasts that perish! Are we to close these paths of investigation also, because some minds have been led by them to a gross materialism? It is not on one subject of inquiry, but in all, that we come speedily to questions which cannot be answered. The result therefore is, that we should never be jealous of research, but always jealous of presumption, — that on all subjects Reason should be warned to keep within the limit of her powers, but from none should Reason be warned away. Men who denounce any particular field of thought are always to be suspected. The presumption is, that valuable things which these men do not like are to be found there. There are many forms of Priestcraft. The same arts, and the same delusions, have been practised in many causes. Sometimes, though perhaps not so often as is popularly supposed, men have been warned off particular branches of physical inquiry, in the supposed interests of Religion. But constantly and habitually, men are now warned from many branches of inquiry, both physical and psychological, in the interests—real enough—of the Positive Philosophy! "Whatever," says Mr. Lewes, "is inaccessible to reason, should be strictly interdicted to research." Here we have the true ring of the old sacerdotal interdicts. Who is to define beforehand what is, and what is not, "inaccessible to reason?" Are we to take such a definition on trust from the priests of this new philosophy? They tell us that all proofs of Mind in the order of the universe, all evidences of purpose, all conceptions of plan or of design, in the history of Creation, are the mere product of special "infirmities" of the human intellect. In opposition to these attempts—come from what quarter they may—to limit arbitrarily the boundaries of knowledge, let us maintain the principle that we never can certainly know what is "inaccessible to reason" until the way of access has been tried. In the highest interests of truth, we must resist any and every interdict against research. The strong presumption is that every philosophy which assumes to issue such an interdict, must have reason to fear inquiry.

On these principles it may be affirmed generally that all subjects are legitimate subjects of reasoning in proportion as they are accessible to research; and that the degree in which any given subject is accessible to research cannot be known until research has been attempted.

Within certain limits it is not open to dispute that the early condition of Mankind is accessible to research. Contemporary history reaches back a certain way. Existing monuments afford their evidence for a considerable distance farther. Tradition has its own province still more remote; and latterly Geology and Archæology have met upon common ground—ground in which Man and the Mammoth have been found together.

It has not, however, been sufficiently observed that the inquiry into the Primitive Condition of Mankind resolves itself into three separate questions,—that is to say, three questions which, though connected with each other, can be, and indeed must be, separately dealt with:—

1st. The Origin of Man considered simply as a Species,—that is to say, the method of his creation or introduction into the world.

2d. The Antiquity of Man, or the time in the geological history and preparation of the globe at which this creation or introduction took place.

3d. His Mental, Moral, and Intellectual Condition when first created.

No doubt the theory as to the Origin of Man at which Sir J. Lubbock glances when he speaks of the "first being worthy to be called a man" (which is obviously the theory that this first man was born from some pre-existing creature not worthy to be so called), is most naturally connected with the farther theory that his mental condition was one of "utter barbarism." But this is not at all a necessary consequence. The first man, however created, may have had special knowledge conveyed to him as well as a special material organization. Special powers of acquiring knowledge he certainly must have had, since we know that these are inseparably connected with the organization which made him "worthy to be called a man." The two questions, therefore, of the Origin of Man, and of his Primitive Condition, are clearly separable. In like manner, as regards Antiquity, the question of Time has no necessary connection either with his Origin or his Primitive Condition.

There is another point connected with this division of the whole subject into three separate questions, which has not perhaps been sufficiently considered, and that is the different degrees of connection which these questions have respectively, with the Mosaic narrative. I have already said that the inquiry as conducted both by Archbishop Whately and Sir J. Lubbock is avowedly conducted on a purely scientific basis. It is in the same light that it will be considered here. But it may be useful to observe in passing, that in regard to some of these questions the Mosaic account of Creation (apart altogether from any suggestions which have been raised as to the allegorical elements it may contain) leaves room, even according to its most literal interpretation, for a much wider latitude of speculation than seems to be generally supposed. As regards the Origin of Man, undoubtedly, the impression conveyed is that the Creation of Man was a special act—which indeed, whatever may have been its method, it must in a sense have been; but, as regards the Primitive Condition of Mankind, it must be remembered that, according to the narrative in Genesis, there never was any generation of men which lived and walked in the primal light. It was the first man who fell. The second man was a murderer. The causes, therefore, of degradation are represented as having begun, so far as the race is concerned, at once; and it is a special peculiarity of the account that those causes are said to have gone on in an accelerating ratio until the Flood. Even after that event there was no immunity from the operation of the same causes, and existing races, therefore, may have passed through stages of any degree of barbarism since the days of Adam without involving any necessary inconsistency whatever with the Mosaic account.

It is farther to be observed that writers on the Primitive Condition of Man are generally guilty of the oversight of forgetting to define the sense in which they use the words "civilized" and "uncivilized." This is a strange oversight on the part of such a logician as Dr. Whately. Sir J. Lubbock naturally enough feels himself relieved from an inconvenient obligation. But implicitly, if not explicitly, the Savage-theory and the reasoning in support of it assume that civilization consists mainly if not exclusively in a knowledge of the arts. Knowledge, for example, or ignorance, of the use of metals, are, as we shall see, characteristics on which great stress is laid. Now, as regards this point, as Whately truly says, the narrative of Genesis distinctly states that this kind of knowledge did not belong to Mankind at first, but was the fruit of subsequent discovery, through the ordinary agency of those mental gifts with which Man at his creation was endowed. It is assumed in the Savage-theory that the presence or absence of this knowledge stands in close and natural connection with the presence or absence of other and higher kinds of knowledge, of which an acquaintance with the metals is but a symbol and a type. Within certain limits this is true, and we may assume, therefore, that in Genesis also, the intimation given on this subject implies that so far as civilization means a command over the powers of nature, Man was left to make his own way, through his powers of reason, and through his instincts of research. Whately has indeed inferred, from the description given of Cain as a tiller of the ground, and of Abel as a keeper of flocks, that the great economic principle of the division of labour was at the first divinely taught to Man. But, if we are to understand this literally, not of tribes tracing their descent from Cain and Abel, but of the individual men who were the third and fourth human beings upon earth, then we must suppose that the possession of domestic animals and acquaintance with artificial cultivation were either divinely communicated to Man, or instinctively discovered by him, at once. It may have been so, and it may be the intention of the narrative to assert it; but, at all events, it is perfectly conceivable, that beyond a knowledge of the simplest arts which were necessary for the sustenance of life, Man's primitive condition may have been a condition of mere childhood.

As regards the third element in the whole question—the element of Time—it is well known that all calculations in regard to it rest upon data respecting which there has always been much doubt and difficulty, and that similar data taken from the three existing versions of the Old Testament,—the Hebrew, the Samaritan, and the Septuagint,—give results which vary from each other, not by years, or even by tens of years, but by many centuries. Where differences exist of such magnitude, no confidence can be felt in any of the results. It seems more than questionable how far the history of Man given in the Old Testament either is, or was intended to be, a complete history, or more than the history of typical men and of typical generations. At all events, it would be worse than idle to deny that this question of Time comes naturally and necessarily within the field of scientific investigation, in so far as science can find a firm foundation for any conclusions in regard to it.

Having already quoted St. Augustine upon the general subject of the desire of knowledge, I cannot close even this cursory reference to the relation in which the Mosaic narrative stands to scientific research, without dwelling for a moment on the very striking passage in which that great man deals with the only account which the world possesses of the history of Creation. St. Augustine was not the man to be dead to all those curious speculations and inquiries which that account excites, and which it does not profess to satisfy. His Confessions, he says, would not be the humble confessions he desires them to be, were he not to confess that as regards many of those questions, he does not understand the sense in which Moses wrote. All the more does he admire his words, "so sublime in their humility, so rich in their reserve" (*alta humiliter, pauca copiose*); then follows (lib. xii. c. 31) a passage which,—considering the age in which it was written, considering also the vague notions entertained by St. Augustine himself, and by all the world in his time, on the rank and importance of the natural sciences,—is surely one of the most remarkable passages ever written by Theologian or Philosopher. "For myself," he says, "I declare boldly, and from the bottom of my heart, that if I were called to write something which was to be invested with supreme authority, I should desire most so to write that my words should include the widest range of meaning, and should not be confined to one sense alone, exclusive of all others, even of some which should be inconsistent with my own. Far from me, O God, be the temerity to suppose that so great a Prophet did not receive from Thy Grace even such a favour! Yes; he had in view and in his spirit, when he traced these words, all that we can ever discover of the truth—even every truth which has escaped us hitherto, or which escapes us still, but which nevertheless may yet be discovered in them." Certain it is, that whatever new views may now be taken of the origin and authorship of the first chapter of Genesis, it stands alone among the traditions of mankind in the wonderful simplicity and grandeur of its words. Specially remarkable—miraculous it really seems to be—is that character of reserve which leaves open to reason all that reason may be able to attain. The meaning of those words seems always to be a meaning a-head of science—not because it anticipates the results of science, but because it is independent of them, and runs, as it were, round the outer margin of all possible discovery.

Having now cleared the ground of some preliminary difficulties which might otherwise have impeded us in a proper access to the subject, I shall proceed in the next Part to deal with the first of the three questions into which that subject is divided—viz. the Origin of Man considered as a Species, in so far as this question appears to be accessible to reason.

PART II.

THE ORIGIN OF MAN.

THE Human Race has no more knowledge or recollection of its own origin than a child has of its own birth. But a child drinks in with its mother's milk some knowledge of the relation in which it stands to its own parents, and as it grows up it knows of other children being born around it. It sees one generation going and another generation coming, so that long before the years of childhood close the ideas of birth and death are alike familiar. Whatever sense of mystery may, in the first dawnings of reflection, have attached to either of these ideas, is soon lost in the familiar experience of the world. The same experience extends to the lower animals—they, too, are born and die. But no such experience ever comes to us casting any light on the Origin of our own Race, or of any other. Some varieties of form are effected in the case of a few animals, by domestication, and by constant care in the selection of peculiarities transmissible to the young. But these variations are all within certain limits; and wherever human care relaxes or is abandoned, the old forms return, and the selected characters disappear. The founding of new forms by the union of different species, even when standing in close natural relation to each other, is absolutely forbidden by the sentence of sterility which Nature pronounces and enforces upon all hybrid offspring. And so it results that Man has never seen the origin of any species. Creation by birth is the only kind of creation he has ever seen; and from this kind of creation he has never seen a new species come. And yet he does know (for this the science of Palæontology has most certainly revealed), that the introduction of new species has been a work carried on constantly and continuously during vast but unknown periods of time. The whole face of animated nature has been changed, not once, but frequently; not suddenly for the most part, perhaps not suddenly in any case, but slowly and gradually, and yet completely. When once this fact is clearly apprehended—whenever we become familiar with the idea that Creation has had a History, we are inevitably led to the conclusion that Creation has also had a Method. And then the further question arises,—What has this method been? It is perfectly natural that men who have any hopes of solving this question should take that supposition which seems the readiest; and the readiest supposition is, that the agency by which new species are created is the same agency by which new individuals are born. The difficulty of conceiving any other compels men, if they are to guess at all, to guess upon this foundation. Such is the origin and genesis of all the theories of Development, of which Mr. Darwin's hypothesis is only the latest form. It is not in itself inconsistent with the Theistic argument, or with belief in the ultimate agency and directing power of a Creative Mind. This is clear, since we never think of any difficulty in reconciling that belief with our knowledge of the ordinary laws of animal and vegetable reproduction. Those laws may be correctly, and can only be adequately, described in the language of religion and theology. "He who is the alone Author and Creator of all things," says the present Bishop of Salisbury, "does not by separate acts of creation give being and life to those creatures which are to be brought forth, but employs His living creatures thus to give effect to His will and pleasure, and as His agents to be the means of communicating life."* The same language might be applied, without the alteration of a word, to the origin of species, if it were indeed true that new kinds as well as new individuals were created by being born. The truth is, that the argument which has so often been employed to elevate our conception of the wisdom hid in secondary causes, is an argument which only gains increasing strength and force in proportion to the number and involution of those causes, and to the extent and scope of their effects. If it does not diminish, but only augments the wonder of Organic Life, that it has been so contrived as to be capable of propagating itself, neither

* Charge, 1867.

would it diminish that wonder, but rather enhance it to an infinite degree, that Organisms should be gifted with the still more wonderful power of developing Forms of Life other and higher than their own. So far, therefore, as belief in a Personal Creator is concerned, the difficulties in the way of accepting this hypothesis are not theological. The difficulties are scientific. The first fundamental difficulty is simply this,—that all the theories of Development ascribe to known causes unknown effects—unknown as regards the times in which we now live, and unknown so far as has hitherto been ascertained in all the past times of which there is any record. It is true that this record—the geological record—is imperfect. But, as Sir

Roderick Murchison has long ago proved, there are parts of that record which are singularly complete, and in those parts we have the proofs of Creation without any indication of Development. The Silurian rocks, as regards Oceanic Life, are perfect and abundant in the forms they have preserved, yet there are no Fish. The Devonian Age followed, tranquilly, and without a break; and in the Devonian Sea, suddenly, Fish appear—appear in shoals, and in forms of the highest and most perfect type. There is no trace of links or transitional forms between the great class of Mollusca and the great class of Fishes. There is no reason whatever to suppose that such forms, if they had existed, can have been destroyed in deposits which have preserved in wonderful perfection the minutest organisms. So much for the Past.

As regards the Present, Organisms are known to reproduce life, but always life which is like their own. And if this likeness admits of degrees of difference, the margin of variety is not known to be ever broad enough for the foundation of a new species. This, too, is remarkable,—that such margin of variety as does ever exist among the offspring of the same parents becomes smaller and smaller in proportion as we rise in the scale of Organic Life. That any organism, therefore, can ever produce another which varies from itself in any truly specific character, is an assumption not justified by any known fact. No organism is ever seen to exert such a power now. There are many indications which tend to show that all organisms have been equally incapable of modification since the earliest monuments of Man. There is no proof that any organism ever did fulfil such functions at any time. The hypothesis is resorted to because of the difficulty of conceiving any method of creation except creation by birth. But this is no adequate standing-ground for a scientific theory. It would be well for those who speculate upon this subject to remember, that whenever a new species or a new class of animal has begun to be, something must have happened which is not in the "ordinary course of nature," as known to us. Something, therefo.·, must have happened which we have a difficulty, probably an insuperable difficulty, in conceiving. If, therefore, the theory of Development can be shown to involve difficulties of conception which are quite as great as those which it professes to remove, then it ceases to have any standing-ground at all. An hypothesis which escapes from particular difficulties by encountering others which are smaller, may be tolerated at least provisionally. But an hypothesis which, to avoid an alternative supposed to be inconceivable, adopts another alternative encompassed by many difficulties quite as great, is not entitled even to provisional acceptance. Now, the difficulties attending the theory of Development, or of creation by birth, attain their maximum in the case of Man. Some of them are referred to in a cursory manner by Dr. Whately. Let us examine them a little nearer.

"Man's place in nature" has long been, and still is, the grand battle-ground of anatomists and physiologists; but the points on which they are disagreed among themselves have not really any importance corresponding to the vehemence with which they have been disputed. The great French anatomist, Cuvier, was of opinion that the distinctions between Man's organism and the organism of the highest among the beasts are of such magnitude and importance, that the human race cannot be classified as belonging to the same "Order" with any other creature, but must be held to constitute an "Order" by itself. In our own time Professor Owen holds the same opinion. Professor Huxley, on the other hand, has undertaken to prove that the anatomical differences between the human frame and the frame of the Gorilla, or Chimpanzee, are not such, either in kind or in degree, as to justify this wide distinction. But he specially limits this conclusion to the differences of physiology, and confesses that, if in defining Man we are to take into account the phenomena of Mind, there is between Man and those beasts which stand nearest to him in anatomy, a difference so wide that it cannot be measured—an "enormous gulf"—"a divergence immeasurable" and "practically infinite." But this last conclusion is really incompatible with the first. There is an inseparable connection between the phenomena of Mind and the phenomena of Organization. They must be taken together, and be interpreted together. The structure of every creature is correlated with the functions which its several parts are fitted to discharge; and the mental character, dispositions, and instincts of the creature are again strictly correlated with these functions. We must accept from anatomists all the facts which anatomy can teach; but the value to be placed on these facts is a very different question. All classification is ideal, and depends on the relative value to be placed on facts which are in themselves indisputable. On this question of the comparative value of anatomical facts we have other facts to go by which do not belong to the science of Physiology. Nature is her own interpreter, and her evidence is clear. Whatever may be the anatomical difference between Man and the Gorilla, that difference is the equivalent, in physical organization, of the whole mental difference between a Gorilla and a Man. This is the measure of value which Nature has set upon the kind and degree of divergence which separates these two Material Forms. Any other measure of value which may be set on that divergence must be founded on an arbitrary and partial selection among the facts of which all sound classification must take account Imperfect as all existing systems of classification are, they are not so bad in the case of any group of the lower animals as to separate organs from the functions they discharge, and from the mental habits which peculiarities of structure merely represent, embody, and subserve. Although the resemblances which have been seized upon for the purpose of grouping together a certain number of animals into Classes, or Families, or Orders, have been for the most part resemblances arbitrarily selected, and have borne no consistent reference to any one standard of comparison throughout the creatures to be arranged, yet those resemblances have not been so arbitrary nor so fallacious as to join together in one common "Order" animals separated from each other in powers and habits by an impassable gulf. Of the eight "Orders" (exclusive of Man) into which Cuvier divided all the animals whose young are suckled (*Mammalia*), one is distinguished from the others by the prehensile character of both feet and hands (*Quadrumana*); another Order is distinguished by the nature of its food (*Carnivora*); the third is distinguished by peculiarities in the production of the young (*Marsupialia*); the fourth and fifth are distinguished by the nature of their teeth (*Rodentia* and *Edentata*); the sixth are distinguished by the texture of their skin (*Pachydermata*); the seventh by peculiarities of the digestive system (*Ruminantia*); and the last by the fish-like form and fish-like habitat of the Whales and Dugongs (*Cetacea*). Now, although it is obvious that no one principle of classification is consistently adhered to in this system,

—although there is no common standard to which they are all referred,—yet, as a matter of fact, the peculiarities chosen are not only the most salient and the most characteristic peculiarities of the animals as a whole, but they are connected with others which run through the whole organism, and with some corresponding similarities of instinct and disposition. But no such defence can be offered for the system which groups Man in the same Order with the Chimpanzee or the Ourang-outang, upon the ground merely that the limbs of those animals are terminated by organs which are anatomically "true feet and true hands;" or because they have the same number of teeth; or because the same primary divisions exist in the structure of the brain.

The difference between the hand of a monkey and the hand of a man may seem small when they are both placed on the dissecting table; but in that difference, whatever it may be, lies the whole difference between an organ limited to the climbing of trees or the plucking of fruit, and an organ which is so correlated with man's inventive genius that by its aid the Earth is weighed, and the distance of the Sun is measured. In like manner let us assume it to be true that the difference between the brain of Man and the brain of the Gorilla may be reduced to a difference of volume, to that visible difference alone, and even as regards volume to a difference in quantity comparatively small. "Cranial capacity' is measured by the cubic inches of space which a skull contains. Professor Huxley tells us,* on the authority of Professor Schaafhausen, that some Hindu skulls have as small a capacity as 46 cubic inches, whilst the largest Gorilla yet measured contained upwards of 35 cubic inches. This represents a difference of volume of less than 11 cubic inches. But the difference between this Hindu skull and the largest European skull (114 cubic inches) amounts, according to the same authority, to no less than 68 cubic inches. Nevertheless the significance set by the facts of nature upon that difference of 11 cubic inches between the Gorilla and the Man, is the difference between an irrational brute confined to some one climate and to some limited area

* Lyell's "Antiquity of Man," p. 84.

of the globe,—which no outward conditions can modify or improve,—and a Being equally adapted to the whole habitable world, with powers, however undeveloped, of comparison, of reflection, of judgment, of reason, with a sense of right and wrong,—and with all these capable of accumulated acquisition, and therefore of indefinite advance. It is not true to affirm that these characteristics stand wholly apart—separated by an "enormous gulf"—from his physical organization. There is an adjustment between these peculiarities of Mind and the special peculiarities of his Frame as nice, and as obvious to sense and reason, as there is between the ferocious disposition of a Tiger and his powerful claws, or between the retractile character of these and his soft and stealthy tread. When anatomists object to erect a separate "Order" for Man on the plea that it is an attempt to reconcile two different orders of ideas,—namely, ideas of anatomical structure, and ideas of mental power,—they are simply refusing to place that value on anatomical differences which nature puts on them. They find no similar difficulty as regards other animals in co-ordinating anatomical structure with mental powers and instincts. The canine teeth of the Carnivora stand in close and consistent relation with their dispositions. The prehensile character of the feet or tail in monkeys is a true and adequate expression of their arboreal habits; and the small and simple brains of the Marsupials (Kangaroos, &c.) are strictly correlated with their low intelligence. We may not—and we do not—understand how these phenomena of Matter and of Mind are thus dependent on each other; but as a fact we see that this dependence is universal, and the distinctions which we found on anatomical structure have their value corroborated and confirmed by close and inseparable correspondences of instinct and intelligence. Man is no exception whatever to this universal law; and any system of classification which places a value on his anatomical peculiarities, separating by an impassable gulf between his Body and his Mind, is a system altogether inconsistent with philosophy. The value set upon any given anatomical peculiarity, or group of peculiarities, in a sound system of classification, ought evidently to correspond as nearly as possible with the value assigned to those peculiarities in the system of nature. The significance of any anatomical feature hinges on the number and variety of other peculiarities to which it stands related. Professor Owen's argument is therefore clearly sound in principle,—that the "consequences" of any such peculiarity must be considered in estimating its systematic value. Take the case of the differences, anatomically small, which distinguish the arms of Man from the arms of a monkey "The consequences," says Professor Owen, "of the liberation of one pair of limbs from all service in station and progression, due to the extreme modification of the other pair for the exclusive discharge of those functions, are greater, and involve a superior number and quality of powers than those resulting from the change of an 'ungulate' (hoofed, one of Cuvier's sub-class divisions) into an 'unguiculate,' or claw-bearing, condition of limb, and they demand therefore an equivalent value in a zoological system."

Accordingly, Professor Owen has attempted to found a system of classification on the degrees of cerebral development, as being the anatomical feature which on the whole stands in the most governing relation to other peculiarities of structure. This proposal has been vehemently contested; but the contest seems to have turned on a point not really vital to the question. Objectors do but aim at proving that all the leading divisions in the brain of Man exist also in the brain of monkeys; and thus, that the difference is reduced to one of volume or quantity alone. But this difference of quantity, relative to the size of the organism, even if no other can be detected by the knife, is correlated with a whole host of other anatomical peculiarities which span the whole breadth of the chasm that yawns between the brutes and Man. These peculiarities must be taken as a whole, in their assemblage, and in their actual connection. The size of Brain is but the index of many other differences, all closely related to one Purpose, and contributing to one result. It is no answer to this argument to say that an equal amount, or even a greater amount, of difference in mere bulk is found to exist between the lowest and the highest human brain, because the fact with which we have to deal is this, that a certain minimum quantity of that mysterious substance is constantly and uniformly associated with all the other anatomical peculiarities of Man. Below that minimum the whole accompanying structure undergoes far more than a corresponding change,—even the whole change between the lowest Savage and the highest Ape. Above that minimum, all subsequent variations in quantity are accompanied by no changes whatever in physical structure. In placing, therefore, a high value—a value in classification of Order, or even of Class—upon the eleven cubic inches of brain-space which lie between the Hindu and the Gorilla, when we place no such value on the sixty-eight cubic inches which lie between the Hindu and Sir Isaac Newton, we are but accepting the evidence of Nature—following where she leads, and classifying according to her award.

The bearing of this conclusion on the Origin of Man is simply this, that in proportion as the difference between Man and the lower animals is properly appreciated in the light of nature, in the same proportion will the difficulty increase of conceiving how the chasm could be passed by any process of Transmutation or Development.

This difficulty is still further increased if we advert for a moment to the direction in which the human frame diverges from the structure of the brutes. It diverges in the direction of greater physical helplessness and weakness. That is to say, it is a divergence which of all others it is most impossible to ascribe to mere "Natural Selection." The unclothed and unprotected condition of the human body, its comparative slowness of foot, the absence of teeth adapted for prehension or for defence, the same want of power for similar purposes in the hands and fingers, the bluntness of the sense of smell, such as to render it useless for the detection of prey which is concealed,—all these are features which stand in strict and harmonious relation to the mental powers of Man. But, apart from these, they would place him at an immense disadvantage in the struggle for existence. This, therefore, is not the direction in which the blind forces of Natural Selection could ever work. The creature "not worthy to be called a man," to whom Sir J. Lubbock has referred as the progenitor of Man, was, *ex hypothesi*, deficient in those mental capacities which now distinguish the lowest of the human race. To exist at all, this creature must have been more animal in its structure; it must have had bodily powers and organs more like those of the beasts. The continual improvement and perfection of these would be the direction of variation most favourable to the continuance of the species. These could not be modified in the direction of greater weakness without inevitable destruction, until first by the gift of reason and of mental capacities of contrivance, there had been established an adequate preparation for the change. The loss of speed or of climbing power which is involved in the fore-arms becoming useless for locomotion, could not be incurred with safety until the brain was ready to direct a hand. The foot could not be allowed to part with its prone or prehensile character until the powers of reason and rêflection had been provided to justify, as it now explains, the erect position and the upward gaze. And so through all the innumerable modifications of form which are the peculiarities of Man, and which stand in indissoluble union with his capacities of thought. The lowest degree of intelligence which is now possessed by the lowest Savage, is not more than enough to compensate him for the weakness of his frame, or to enable him to maintain successfully the struggle for existence. With many Savages it is a hard struggle, despite senses of sight and hearing trained by necessity so as almost to approach the instincts of the lower animals; despite also all those powers of reasoning which, however low, are yet peculiar to himself, and separate him, as is confessed, by an impassable gulf from the highest of the beasts. Many of the Aborigines of Australia could do no more at times than support a precarious existence by scraping up roots, and eating snakes and other reptiles. The rotten blubber of a dead whale cast upon the beach was, and is often, not only a luxury and a feast, but deliverance from actual starvation. Sir

J. Lubbock's theory is, that in these Savages we see something rather above than under the primitive condition of Mankind. But it may be safely said that a very small diminution of mental capacity below that of an Australian Savage, would render Man's characteristic structure incompatible with the maintenance of his existence in most, if not in all, of the countries where he is actually found. If that frame was once more bestial, it may have been better adapted for a bestial existence. But it is impossible to conceive how it could ever have emerged from that existence by virtue of Natural Selection. Man must have had human proportions of mind before he could afford to lose bestial proportions of body. If the change in mental power came simultaneously with the change in physical organization, then it was all that we can ever know or understand of a new creation. There is no ground whatever for supposing that ordinary generation has been the agency employed, seeing that no effects similar in kind are ever produced by that agency, so far as is known to us. The theory of Transmutation in all its forms, even as applied to the lower animals, is exposed to many difficulties greater than those which it professes to remove. But as applied to Man, those difficulties are accumulated to an incalculable degree. Most of them, too, are altogether of a special kind, because the divergence which ordinary generation is supposed to have produced in the case of Man is a divergence, to use Professor Huxley's words, "immeasurable—practically infinite."

It needs only to be added to this sketch, that such as Man now is, Man, so far as we yet know, has always been. Two skeletons at least have been found respecting which there is strong ground for believing that they belong to the very earliest human race which lived in Northern Europe. I defer any reference to the probable epoch of time when those skeletons were clothed with flesh and blood. This belongs to the next division of our subject, which is the Antiquity as distinguished from the Origin of Man. Suffice it here to say that although one of those skeletons indicates a coarse, perhaps even what we should call—as we might fairly call some living specimens of our race—a brutal man, yet even this skeleton is in all its proportions strictly human. Its cranial capacity indicates a volume of brain, and some peculiarities of shape not materially different from many skulls of Savage races now living. The other skeleton, respecting which the evidence of extreme antiquity is the strongest, is not only perfectly human in all its proportions, but its skull has a cranial capacity not inferior to that of many modern Europeans. This most ancient of all known human skulls is so ample in its dimensions that it might have contained the brains of a philosopher. So conclusive is this evidence against any change whatever in the specific characters of Man since the oldest

Human Being yet known was born, that Professor Huxley pronounces it to be clearly indicated "that the first traces of the primordial stock whence Man has proceeded need no longer be sought, by those who entertain any form of the doctrine of progressive development, in the newest tertiaries,"—(that is, in the oldest deposit yet known to contain human remains at all.) "But," he adds, "they may be looked for in an epoch more distant from the age of those tertiaries than that is from us."* So far, therefore, the evidence is on the side of the originality of Man as a species, nay, even as a Class by himself, separated by a gulf practically immeasurable from all the crea-

* Lyell, "Antiquity of Man," p. 89.

tures that are, or that are known ever to have been, his contemporaries in the world. In possession of this ground, we can wait for such further evidence in favour of Transmutation as may be brought to. light. Meanwhile at least we are entitled to remain incredulous, remembering, as Professor Phillips has said, that "everywhere we are required by the hypothesis to look somewhere else; which may fairly be interpreted to signify that the hypothesis everywhere fails in the first and most important step. How is it conceivable that the second stage should be everywhere preserved, but the first nowhere?"*

* "Life—the Origin and Succession," by Professor John Phillips.

PART III.

THE ANTIQUITY OF MAN.

IN passing from the subject of Man's Origin to the subject of his Antiquity, we pass from almost total darkness to a question which is comparatively accessible to reason and open to research. Evidence bearing upon this question may be gathered along several different walks of science, and these are all found tending in one direction, and pointing to one general result. First comes the evidence of History, embracing under that name all literature, whether it professes to record events, or does no more than allude to them in poetry and song. Then comes Archæology, the evidence of Human Monuments, belonging to times or races whose voice, though not silenced, has become inarticulate to us. Piecing on to this evidence, comes that which Geology has recently afforded from human remains associated with the latest physical changes on the surface and in the climates of the globe. Then comes the evidence of Language, founded on the facts of Human Speech, and the laws which regulate its development and growth. And lastly, there is the evidence afforded by the existing physical structure, and the existing geographical distribution of the various Races of

Mankind. According as we may have made one or other of these great branches of inquiry our favourite pursuit, we may be disposed to place a different estimate on their comparative value. But perhaps we shall not go far wrong if we arrange them in the order here given, as the order in which they stand relatively to the directness and certainty of the testimony they afford.

One distinction, however, it is important to bear in mind. Chronology is of two kinds, —first, Time measurable by years,—and secondly, Time measurable only by an ascertained order or succession of events. The one may be called Time-absolute, the other Time-relative. Now, among all the sciences which afford us evidence on the

Antiquity of Man, one, and one only, gives us any knowledge of Time-absolute; and that is History. From all the others we can gather only the less definite information of Time-relative. They can tell us of nothing more than of the order in which certain events took place. But of the length of interval between those events, neither Archæology, nor Geology, nor Ethnology can tell us anything. Even History, that is, the records of Written Documents, carries us back to times of which no contemporary account remains, and the distance of which in years from any known epoch is, and must be, a matter of conjecture. No other history than the Hebrew History even professes to go back to the Creation of Man, or to give any account of the events which connect existing generations with the first Progenitor of their Race. And of that History, the sole object appears to be, to give in outline the order of such transactions as had a special bearing on Religious Truth, and on the course of Spiritual Belief. The intimations given in the earlier chapters of the Book of Genesis on all matters of purely secular interest, are incidental only, and exceedingly obscure. And yet it is not a total silence. Enough is said to indicate how much there lay beyond and outside of the narrative which is given. The dividing of the Tribes of the Gentiles among the descendants of Japheth,* conveys the idea of movements and operations which probably occupied long

* Gen. x. 2, 5.

intervals of time, and many generations of men. The same impression must arise from the condensed abstract given of the origin and growth of communities capable of building such cities as Resen and Calah and Nineveh are described to be.* In the genealogy of the family of Shem, we have a list of names, which are names and nothing more to us. It is a genealogy which neither does, nor professes to do, more than to trace the order of succession among a few families only out of the millions then already existing in the world. Nothing but this order of succession is given, nor is it at all certain that this order is consecutive or complete. Nothing is told us of all that lay behind

* Gen. x. 11, 12.

that curtain of thick darkness, in front of which these names are made to pass. And yet there are, as it were, momentary liftings, through which we have glimpses of great movements which were going on, and had long been going on, beyond. No shapes are distinctly seen. Even the direction of those movements can be only guessed. But voices are heard which are as the voices of many nations. The very first among the descendants of Noah whose individuality and personality is clear to us,—the very first whose doings can be brought into relation with events otherwise known or recognizable in the History of Man,—is introduced in a manner which reveals the fact that different races of the human family had then already been long established and widely spread. The memorable and mysterious journey which brought Terah into Haran on his way to Canaan,* was a journey beginning in that ancient home, Ur, already known as "of the Chaldees." And when the great figure of his son Abraham appears upon the scene, we find ourselves already in the presence of the Monarchy of Egypt, and of the advanced civilization of the Pharaohs. In the same narrative, on another side, we come into the presence of one of those great military Kingdoms of the East which in succession occupy so large a space in the history of the ancient world. Chedorlaomer, with his tributary Princes, was then

* Gen. xi. 31.

the ruler of nations capable of waging wars of conquest at great distances from the seat of their government, and the centre of their power. We see in him therefore the Sovereign of a long-established and powerful race. And yet these migrations and wars of Abraham stand, if not at the very beginning of History, at least at the very beginning of Historical Chronology. They mark the very earliest date in the history of Man, on which, within moderate limits of discrepancy, all chronologists are agreed. That date may be fixed at 2,000 B.C. This is the boundary, in looking backwards, of Time-absolute. All beyond, is Time-relative. We have, indeed, other evidence of an historical character to show that the Monarchy of Egypt had been founded long before the time of Abraham. But how long, is a question on which there is the widest discrepancy of opinion. The most moderate computation, however, carries the foundation of that Monarchy as far back as 700 years before the visit of the Hebrew Patriarch. Some of the best German scholars hold that there is evidence of a much longer chronology. But seven centuries before Abraham is the estimate of Mr. R. Stuart Poole, of the British Museum, who is one of the very highest authorities, and certainly the most cautious, upon questions of Egyptian chronology. This places the beginning of the Pharaohs in the twenty-eighth century B.C. But according to Ussher's interpretation of the Hebrew Pentateuch, the twenty-eighth century B.C. would be some 400 years before the Flood. On the other hand, a difference of 800 years is allowed by the chronology which is founded on the Septuagint Version of the Scriptures. But the fact of this difference tells in two ways. A margin of variation amounting to eight centuries between two versions of the same document, is a variation so enormous, that it seems to cast complete doubt on the whole system of interpretation on which such computations of time are based. And yet it is more than questionable whether it is possible to reconcile the known order of events with even this larger estimate of the number of years. It is true that, according to this larger estimate, the Flood would be carried back about four and a half centuries beyond the beginning of the Pharaohs. But is this enough? The founding of a Monarchy is not the beginning of a race. The people amongst whom such Monarchies arose must have grown and gathered during many generations. Nor is it in regard to the peopling of Egypt alone that this difficulty meets us in the face. The existence in the days of Abraham of such an organized government as that of Chedorlaomer, shows that 2,000 years B.C. there flourished in Elam, beyond Mesopotamia, a nation which even now would be ranked among "the Great Powers." And if nations so great had thus arisen, altogether unnoticed in the Hebrew narrative—if we are left to gather as best we may from other sources, all our knowledge of their origin and growth, how much more is this true of far distant lands over which the advancing tide of human population had rolled, or was then rolling its mysterious wave? If the most ancient and the most sacred literature in the world tells us so little of the early history of the men who lived and flourished on the banks of the Euphrates, the Tigris, or the Nile, what information can we expect to find in it respecting those who were probably already settled on the Indus and the Ganges, or were spreading along the banks of the Brahmaputra and of the Yellow River? What of those tribes who were following the Volga and the Oxus, or the Danube and the Rhine? What of that vast Continent whose secrets are being revealed at last only in our own day—the Continent of Africa? When and how did that Negro Race begin, which is both one of the most ancient and one of the most strongly marked among the varieties of Man? And what again can we learn from Genesis of the peopling of the New World? When did Man first come upon the inland seas of America, and follow the great rivers which fall into the Gulf of Mexico?

It is not possible to suppose that some 450 years before the foundation of the Egyptian Monarchy is a period long enough to account even for the few facts which are implied in the Mosaic narrative itself, respecting the dispersion and geographical distribution of Mankind. And to those facts must be added others resting on evidence which is still historical. There is another civilization which appears to have been almost as ancient as that of Egypt, and which has been far more enduring. The authentic records of the Chinese Empire are said to begin in the twenty-fourth century B.C. — that is, more than 300 years before the time of Abraham.* They begin, too, apparently with a Kingdom already established, with a capital city, and with a settled government.† Yet this civilization first appears at the farthest extremity

* "The Chinese;" G. T. T. Meadows, p. 34.

† Since this passage was published I have been favoured with an interesting letter from the Rev. James Legge, who has spent many years as a Missionary in China, and has published valuable editions of the Historical works of the Chinese.

of Asia, separated by many thousands of miles, and by some of the most impassable regions of the world, from the cradle of the Human Race, and from the country where Noah and his family were saved. Such facts seem to point to one or other of two conclusions—either that the Flood must have happened at a period in the history of Man vastly earlier than any that has been usually supposed, or else that the Flood destroyed only a small portion of the Human Family. That the Deluge affected only a small portion

It is this gentleman's opinion that the Chinese Tribe was only beginning to grow into a kingdom about 2,000 B.C. and, that 1,200 years later, the kingdom did not extend nearly so far south as the Yang-tsze river. The general conclusion to which these dates point, is not, I think, materially affected by this somewhat shortened estimate of Chinese Historical Chronology.

of the globe which is *now habitable* is almost certain. But this is quite a different thing from supposing that the Flood affected only a small portion of the world which was *then inhabited.* The wide, if not the universal prevalence among the heathen nations, of a tradition preserving the memory of some such great catastrophe, has always been considered to indicate recollection carried by descent from the surviving few. And this tradition seems to be curiously strong and definite among tribes which are now separated by half the circumference of the globe from the region affected by the Flood. At all events this is clear, that the difficulty of reconciling the narrative of Genesis with an indefinitely older date is a very small difficulty indeed, as compared with the difficulty of reconciling it with a very limited destruction of the Human Race. The evidence for a higher antiquity of Man is derived from countries in comparatively close proximity with those which, under any possible supposition as to the area of a Deluge, must have been then submerged. On the other hand, we have seen how utterly uncertain and how enormously different are the chronologies which profess to be founded on the Pentateuch. They all involve suppositions as to the principle of interpretation, and as to the import of words descriptive of descent, which are in the highest degree doubtful, and which it is evident cannot be applied consistently throughout. Thus, when we read* of Canaan, the grandson of Noah, that he "begat Sidon, his firstborn, and Heth," we seem to have the names of individual men; but, when it is immediately added that he also "begat the Jebusite, and the Amorite, and the Girgasite, and the Hivite, and the Arkite, and the Sinite," &c. &c., it is clear that we are dealing not with single generations, but with a condensed abstract of the origin and growth of Tribes. No definite information is given in such abstracts as to the lapse of time. The chronology of changes not specially included in the narrative, can only be gathered from the general character of the events described. And that general character is such as fully to corroborate the evidence we have

* Gen. x. 15—18.

from other sources—that long before the Call of Abraham, that is to say, long before the twentieth century B.C., the Human Race had been increasing and multiplying on the earth from such ancient days that in many regions, far removed from the centre of their dispersion, great nations had arisen, powerful and civilized governments had been established.

So far, then, we have the light of History shining with comparative clearness over a period of 2,000 years before the Christian era. Beyond that we have a twilight tract of time which may be roughly estimated at 700 years—a period of time lying in the dawn of History, at the very beginning of which we can dimly see that there were already Kings and Princes on the earth.

But this is the outer margin of Time-absolute. No farther, with even an approximation to the truth, can we measure the order of events by the lapse of years.

But there is a point at which the evidence of Archæology begins before the evidence of History has closed. There is a border-land where both kinds of evidence are found together, or rather, where some testimony exists of which it is difficult to say whether it is the testimony of written documents or of the inarticulate monuments of Man. It was the habit of one of the most ancient nations in the world to record all events in the form of pictorial representation. Their domestic habits, their foreign wars, their religious beliefs, are thus all presented to the eye. And one of the questions on which this testimony bears is a question of paramount importance in determining the antiquity of the Human Family. That question is not the rise of Kingdoms, but the origin of Races. The varieties of Man are a great mystery. The physical differences which these varieties involve may be indeed, and often are, much exaggerated. Yet, these differences are distinct, and we are naturally impelled to ask When and How did they begin? These are two separate questions; but the one bears upon the other. The question When stands before the question How. The fundamental problem to be solved is this: Can such varieties have descended from a single stock? And if they can, then must not a vast and indefinite lapse of time have been occupied in the gradual development of divergent types? On this question we have no datum on which to reason, unless we can ascertain how far back in Time-absolute these divergences had already become established. Now, this is the datum which Egypt gives us. In one of the most perfect of the paintings which have been preserved to us, a great Egyptian monarch is symbolically represented as ruling with the power of life and death over subject races: and these are depicted with accurate and characteristic likeness. Conspicuous in this group is one figure, painted to the life both in form and colour, which proves that the race which departs most widely from the European type, had then acquired exactly the same characters which mark it in the present day. The Negro kneels at the feet of Sethos I., in the same attitude of bondage and submission which typifies only too faithfully the enduring servitude of his race. The blackness of colour, the woolliness of hair, the flatness of nose, the projection of the lips, which are so familiar to us,—all these had been fully established and developed thus early in the known history of the world. And this was about 1,400 years before the Christian era—that is to say, more than 3,200 years ago. I am informed by Professor Lepsius (through the kindness of Mr. Poole) that there are some still earlier representations of the Negro—referable to the "Twelfth Dynasty," or to about 1,900 B.C. In these it is curious that the Negro colour is strongly marked, but not the Negro feature. This, however, may be due to the unskilfulness of early art, or to the fact, too often forgotten, that some African tribes —as, for example, the Nubians—have not the low flat nose or the projecting lips. Nor is this the whole evidence afforded by the Egyptian pictures. At periods not much later in the history, we have elaborate representations of battles with Negro nations,—representations which go far to show that the race was then more able to maintain a contest with other races than it has ever been in recent times. And of this a further proof is to be found in the fact, that at a period

at least 2,000 years B.C.—that is about the

time of Abraham—mention is made in hieroglyphic writings of Black or Negro troops being raised by an Egyptian king, to assist him in the prosecution of a great war.*

Since, then, the Negro race was already, in the days of Abraham, just what it is now, what is the time we must allow for the development of this variety of Man, supposing it to have descended from a common stock? We have absolutely no measurement of time by which to estimate the growth of such varieties. We know that changes of climate and of food do

* Drawings by the skilful hands of Mr. Bonomi are given on p. 101 and on the Frontispiece in illustration of the facts stated in the text. They are taken from an Egyptian temple at Beyt-el-Welee, in Nubia, of the reign of Rameses II., son and successor of Sethos I.

produce upon Mankind some modifications of colour, and of features. But we know also that such changes are extremely slow. Colour is in all the lower animals one of the least constant—that is to say, one of the most variable, — of external characters; and under circumstances of domestication changes of colour are sometimes sudden, and are connected with causes altogether unknown. But we have no evidence to show that human colour is liable to changes of a like kind. On the contrary, all experience seems to point to the conclusion that varieties of complexion can only be established very gradually, and we have no absolute proof that a change from white to negro blackness is pcssible at all. A very able and ingenious writer, whose work is unfortunately anonymous,* but whose opinions are endorsed by the high authority of Mr. Poole, has assumed that this change is not within the compass of any natural causes, and cannot be accounted for by any lapse of time. On this as well as on other grounds he adopts the theory that Adam was the progenitor of the white races only; and that before the creation of Adam, the Black Race had been established in the Continent of Africa. He maintains that in the Mosaic narrative, contrary to the usual interpretation, there are clear indications of the existence of pre-Adamite races. This theory undoubtedly explains

* "Genesis of the Earth and of Man."

one passage in Genesis, which seems otherwise wholly unintelligible, namely, that in which mention is made of unions between the "Sons of God" and the daughters of men. Our author affirms that for the "Sons of God" we ought to substitute as the true meaning in the original, "the servants of the gods," or in other words the idolatrous races of the world. In like manner the daughters of men should be translated, "the daughters of the Adamite." The passage would thus refer to intermarriages between the children of Adam and the pre-existing idolatrous nations of the world. It is true also that this theory would remove or diminish some other difficulties attending the received interpretation. But on the other hand the

Unity of Mankind is so deeply interwoven with the fundamental doctrines of Christianity, as hitherto universally understood, that the new difficulties raised are far greater than those which would be thus removed. No doubt it may be said that the Unity of Mankind as a species, does not necessarily depend upon descent from a single pair; and it is true that this Unity is a matter of fact which cannot under any hypothesis be denied; because we know that the barrier of hybrid barrenness which nature sets against the mixture of different species does not impede the amalgamation of even the most diverse varieties of Man. It is therefore certain that in this sense, which involves the full possession of a common nature, "God hath made of one blood all nations of men for to dwell on all the face of the earth." It is of course conceivable that this full community of nature may have been given by the Creator to two or more original pairs. But all the evidence of science tends to the conclusion that each well-marked species has spread from some one centre of creation, and presumably from a single pair. There is no clashing between this evidence and the testimony of Revelation as that testimony has hitherto been interpreted. Strongly marked as the varieties of Man now are, the variation is strongest in respect to colour, which in all organisms is notoriously the most liable to modification and to change. And in this feature of colour it is remarkable that we have every possible variety of tint from the fairest to the blackest races, so that the one extreme passes into the other by small and insensible gradations. As regards structure, the differences between different varieties of Man are comparatively trifling, and it may safely be affirmed that all the efforts of anatomists and physiologists who have been most determined to magnify every point of variation, have utterly failed to render it impossible or improbable that all men have had a common ancestor. But in exact proportion as we hold to this conclusion as the only satisfactory explanation of the Unity of Man, must we be prepared to accept the high probability, if not the certainty, of the very great antiquity of the Race.

Next comes the science of Language, of which those who have made it a special study affirm, that it affords the most conclusive evidence of all, that the articulate voice of Man has been sounding in the world during vast though indefinite periods of time. "The evidence of language," says Professor Max Müller, "is irrefragable, and it is the only evidence worth listening to with regard to ante-historical periods." And what does this evidence go to prove? Let us take one example. "There was a time," says the same author, "when the ancestors of the Celts, the Germans, the Slavonians, the Greeks, and Italians, the Persians and Hindus, were living together beneath the same roof—separate from the ancestors of the Semitic (Hebrew) and Turanian races."* The principle on which the evidence of language is interpreted is very simple. The sounds or words by which men designate things are for the most part arbitrary, and therefore conventional. The sign and the thing signified have no natural or necessary connection. The names of a very few animals may be imitations of their voice. No argument, for example, could be founded on the word Cuckoo being used by the most diverse tribes to designate a bird which sounds these two syllables in its cry. But such cases are very rare even in the names of beasts. Wherever the same thing is denoted by the same word, and where there is no natural connection between them, there

* "Chips from a German Workshop," vol. i. pp. 63, 64.

must have been once a common understanding amongst men who dwelt together, as to the meaning of that sound. And when this common understanding is found to affect the nearest relationships of life, and the animals domesticated in primeval times, the evidence of ancient consanguinity is complete. In this case "the terms for God, for house, for father, mother, son, daughter, for dog and cow, for heart and tears, for axe and tree, identical in all the Indo-Germanic words, are like the watchwords of soldiers." But when was it that the fathers of nations now so far apart as Germans and Hindus were living together under one roof? This is a question which, in the terms of Time-absolute, no man can answer. Only we know that before the time of Abraham the languages of those great leading stocks must have been nearly as far apart as they are now. Professor Max Müller is of opinion that to the Hymns of the Vedas a later date cannot be assigned than 1,200 B.C. Homer and Hesiod are in all probability referable to a later date, but not so much later as to cast any doubt on the conclusion that both Greek and Sanskrit were then perfectly developed. Those who have studied the growth of languages, and the mysterious laws by which that growth is regulated, are lost in conjecture as to the lapse of time which may probably have been required to account for the wonderful creations of Human Speech.

Next comes the evidence of Geology, which

only in very recent years has been found to speak with any distinctness upon the question of Man's Antiquity. Not that there is any change in the general bearing of that evidence as it stood before. There is none whatever. The evidence of Geology has always been, that among all the creatures which have in succession been formed to live upon this earth, and to enjoy it, Man is the latest born. This great fact is still the fundamental truth in the History of Creation: that history, as Geology has revealed it, has been a history of successive Creations, and of successive Destructions,—Old Forms of Life perishing, and New Forms appearing, so that the whole face of nature has been many times renewed. But until very lately it was supposed that these vast cycles of change had been finally completed before Man appeared. And as regards fresh creations this supposition is still supported by the testimony of science. So far as we yet know, no New Form of Life has been created since the Highest Form was made. But it now appears that since that event many Old Forms have died. The Cycles of Creation had closed, but not the Cycles of Destruction. Of itself, it might be supposed that this fact has little bearing upon the question of Time. The extinction of some noxious animals in particular parts of the globe, as for example in our own country, has taken place within the period of history, and some few species of wingless birds, as the Dodo and the Great Auk, have been destroyed in very recent times. But these have been extinctions effected through the agency of Man. What is now proved is that a whole group or fauna of great quadrupeds have utterly perished since Man appeared. And the causes of this destruction seem to have been of the same kind as the causes which in all former ages had produced similar results—viz., great changes in the climates of the globe, and great movements affecting the configuration of its surface. In these last circumstances lies the real stress of the evidence derived from the new discoveries. It is conceivable that old kinds of Elephant and Rhinoceros may have roamed over Northern Europe when its surface and its climate were the same as they now are. It is less probable that the small streams which now exist in England should have harboured herds of Hippopotami. But the position in which the remains of these great animals are found indicates that since they flourished there have been considerable changes in physical geography. It indicates, too, that a great change of climate has accompanied certain changes in the configuration of land and sea. I know no better example of the evidence to this effect than one which is very easily accessible in our own country. We have only to go down to the pleasant shores of Devon, and to one of the pleasantest spots upon those shores—the south-western promontory of Torbay. Overhanging the little harbour of Brixham, where two hundred years ago William of Orange landed, there is a steep limestone hill, at the foot and on the face of which the houses of the town are built. Close to the summit a few years ago a cavernous hollow was discovered. It extends a considerable distance through the limestone rocks, and no one who goes through it can fail to see that it has once been the bed of a stream. The smooth surfaces worn by the long action of running water are perfectly preserved, and the rounded pebbles which were found in the bed of this ancient stream are additional evidences of the fact. Now let any one stand at the entrance, or at the exit of this cavern and cast his eye on the surrounding landscape. Whence can this stream have flowed, and whither? The hill is now separated from all higher ground by valleys which are at least sixty feet below the level of the cave. It is evident at a glance that the whole physical geography of the country must have been different, when running water channelled this limestone hill. Yet in this cave the works of Man, flint arrow-heads and knives, were found, along with the bones of the Elephant, the Rhinoceros, the Bear, the Hyæna, and the Reindeer. As regards one of these animals, the whole leg was found together, showing that the bones had been covered with flesh when they were carried by the stream. This is only one case out of very many which have now been discovered in various parts of Europe.

I need not here go farther into detail as regards this kind of evidence. Suffice it to say, that all the facts tend to these three general conclusions: 1st, that Man appeared in Northern Europe at a time when it was covered with great quadrupeds now wholly extinct; 2d, that the surface of the Earth has since that period been subjected to modifications, which imply great changes in physical geography; and 3d, that the period when those animals flourished, and when Man co-existed with them, was one when a colder climate prevailed. Now no one conclusion of geological science is more firmly established than this, that there was a time, comparatively very recent, when an Arctic climate prevailed far down into latitudes which are now temperate; and when a great part of Northern Europe and of our own islands was submerged under a Glacial Sea.) This sea was ploughed by floating icebergs, which as they melted dropped their rocks and boulders upon the bottom. That bottom has since been raised again into dry land, and these boulders now interrupt the drainer in cultivated fields, and strew the surface of our wildest moors. Many concurring indications go far to prove that it was when this Glacial Period had nearly passed away, when a milder climate was beginning to prevail over the land which we now know, that Man also began to find his way into Northern Europe. There he sought his living among herds of animals, of which the greater number are now extinct and a few remain only in those regions which are still Arctic. This is the order of events as we can read it with tolerable certainty in the language of Time-relative. But we have little means of knowing what relation this order of events bears to Time-absolute. It is still disputed among Geologists how far the causes of geological change were once more intense in their action than they are now. It is quite certain that during the passing away of a glacial climate, the cutting power of rivers must have been intensified by the increasing rapidity with which ice and snows were melted. There are also facts connected with the position in which remains of the extinct animals are often found, which cannot, in my opinion, be explained, except by violent and sudden action since or during the period of their entombment. Great caves, packed closely from floor to roof with the bones of the Hippopotamus and Rhinoceros ; other caves, equally full of the bones of extinct Oxen, are proofs of some diluvial action of which Man has had no experience in historic times. But, even allowing for the greater activity of geological causes, the time required for such changes of climate has in all probability been very great. And when we consider that many of these evidences of Geology apply to the New World as well as to the Old, we cannot fail to see that the proofs of a very high antiquity for the Human Race are proofs of a cumulative character, gathered along several different paths of investigation, and all tending to one general result.

That result, however, is necessarily indefinite, and cannot be expressed in years. Of the evidence from the dispersion of the Human Race, it may be fairly said that we do not know how rapidly Man may have spread when the beasts of the chase were yet unacquainted with his destructive powers, when they probably swarmed in innumerable herds, and when from their tameness they must have fallen an easy prey. Of the evidence from Language it may again be said that we do not know how rapidly the forms of human speech may have altered among tribes wandering and unsettled, rapidly changing place, and as rapidly accommodating themselves to new scenes and new necessities. In like manner, of the evidence from Geology it may be said that we do not know how rapidly changes of climate may have been effected if the agencies which determine the distribution of Sea and Land were more active than they have been in historic times. All these are pleas in mitigation of extreme demands in point of time, and they are pleas which may be fairly urged. But when all due allowance has been made for the considerations to which they point, there remains a weight and concurrence of authority in favour of a long chronology which grows and increases in the minds of all who have studied each one of the separate branches of inquiry.

For my own part I see no reason to be

jealous of the conclusions of science in this matter. The question is, after all, a small one. It is a question of a few thousand years more or less; and thousands of years are as less than seconds in the Creative Days. The estimates of Time which have been given us by Geology have been compared with the estimates of Space given us by Astronomy. But there is an important difference. There is no visible limit to Astronomical Space. The apparent magnitude of the largest of the Heavenly Bodies shows that millions of miles are quantities inappreciable even to our eyes, and that worlds are scattered like dust through illimitable depths. But it is not so with Geological Time. Its periods are indeed very long, but the beginning of them can be seen.

It is not a boundless ocean, it is only a very broad sea. On the other side of it there rise the mountains of a Lifeless Land. Successive creations mark the distance between us and them, and although we cannot say what that distance is, we can say that it is a finite distance—that beyond a boundary which we can see, the world was not a world such as we now live in, but a world comparatively "without form and void." The question of Man's Antiquity involves no attempt to measure the breadth of this great space, but only the breadth of a little bay or creek, close to the shores on which we are now standing. Be this breadth greater or smaller by one, two, or three, or four, or five, or ten thousand years, its *relative* place in the great Tracts of Creative Time undergoes no change whatever. Man is the latest work. Recent discoveries have thrown no doubt on this, but, on the contrary, have all tended to confirm it. I know of no one moral or religious truth which depends on a short estimate of Man's antiquity. On the contrary, a high estimate of that antiquity is of great value in its bearing upon another question much more important than the question of time can ever be—viz., the question of the Unity of the Human Race. We must indeed be very cautious in identifying the interests of Religion with any interpretation (however certain we may have hitherto assumed it to be) of the language of Scripture upon subjects which are accessible to scientific research. We know from past experience how foolish and how futile it is to do so. But unquestionably the Unity of the Human Race, in respect to origin, is not easily separated from some principles which are of high value in our understanding both of moral duty and of religious truth. And precisely in proportion as we value our belief in that Unity ought we to be ready and willing to accept any evidence on the question of Man's Antiquity. The older the Human Family can be proved to be, the more possible and probable it is that it has descended from a single pair. My own firm belief is that all scientific evidence is in favour of this conclusion; and I regard all new proofs of the Antiquity of Man as tending to establish it on a firmer basis.

PART IV.

MAN'S PRIMITIVE CONDITION.

AS the question of Man's Origin is different from the question of his Antiquity, and as the Antiquity of Man is a different question from his Primitive Condition, so again the last question includes within itself several different matters of inquiry. There is first the question, What consciousness had Primeval Man of Moral Obligation, and what communion with his Creator? Next there is the question, What were his innate powers of Intellect or

Understanding? And, thirdly, there is the question, What was his condition in respect to Knowledge, whether as the result of intuition, or as the result of teaching? It is a fatal fault in the discussion of this subject, as conducted both by Archbishop Whately and by Sir J. Lubbock, that these distinctions are either not seen or not distinctly kept in view. Perhaps, indeed, it may be thought that the Savage-theory is independent of such close analysis. But this is by no means the case. The distinction between the possession of Faculties capable of acquiring knowledge, and the possession of knowledge actually acquired, is a fundamental distinction. Not less fundamental is the distinction between a creature who is morally good but intellectually uninformed, and a creature who is both ignorant and vicious. Sir J. Lubbock speaks of Primeval Man as having been in a condition of "utter barbarism." But no one, speaking philosophically, has a right to use such terms as "barbarism" and "civilization" without some definition of their meaning. What were those Faculties which made the first creature who possessed them "worthy to be called a Man?" A Mind capable of reason, disposed to reason, and able to acquire, to accumulate, and to transmit knowledge,—this is the distinctive attribute of Man. The first Being "worthy to be so called," must have had such a mind. But it could not properly be said of such a Being, on the ground merely of his ignorance of mechanical arts, that he was in a condition of "utter barbarism," if he were at the same time conscious of moral obligations and obedient to them. It is, of course, open to a theorist to assume that the First Man was both ignorant and bad, or that the sense of right and wrong was rudimentary and wholly uninformed. But all I desire to point out here is, that there is no necessary connection between a state of mere childhood in respect to knowledge, and a state of "utter barbarism"—words which, if they have any definite meaning at all, imply the lowest moral, as well as the lowest intellectual condition. Consequently no proof, if proof there be, that Primeval Man was ignorant of the industrial arts can afford the smallest presumption that he was also ignorant of duty oı ignorant of God. This is a fundamental objection to the whole scope of Sir J. Lubbock's argument. It interposes an impassable gulf between his premises and his conclusion.

But there is another objection equally fundamental. Traces or remains of barbarism, properly so called, that is, traces of customs savage or immoral, in the usages of civilized nations, may be an indication of the fact that those nations, or the races from which they sprang, have passed through a stage of barbarism. But it affords no presumption whatever that barbarism was the Primeval Condition of Man, any more than the traces of Feudalism in the laws of modern Europe prove that feudal principles were born with the Human Race. All such customs may have been, and as many think, probably have been, not Primeval but Medieval, that is to say, the result of time and of development, and that development a development of corruption. To assume that they were original, or that they were even better or less barbarous than others which preceded them, is to assume the whole question in dispute. Yet this assumption runs through all Sir J. Lubbock's arguments. Wherever a brutal or savage custom prevails it is at once assumed to be a sample of the original condition of Mankind. And this in the teeth of facts which prove that many of such customs not only may have been, but must have been, the result of corruption. Take cannibalism as one of these. Sir J. Lubbock seems to admit that this loathsome practice was not primeval, probably because he considers it as unnatural.* And so it is,—that is to say, it is against the better nature of Man; but the fact of its existence proves that within the limits of that nature there are elements liable to perversions even so horrible as this. And so we come upon the fact of the two natures of Man, and of the power of the worst parts of his nature to overcome the best. It is thus that customs the most cruel and depraved become established. But if this be the explanation, and the only possible explanation, of cannibalism, is it not evident that this may also be the explanation of other customs which are violent and horrible

* "Prehistoric Times," p. 371.

only in a less degree? — Cruel rites of worship, and savage customs as regards marriage and the relation of the sexes, come under the same category.* Cannibalism is only an extreme case of a general law, and it is a crucial test of the fallacy of a whole class of arguments commonly assumed by those who support the Savage-theory respecting the Primeval Condition of Mankind.

On the other hand, I think it cannot be denied that the argument of Whately is equally defective in failing to recognise the essential distinctions to which I have referred.

* Much stress is laid on these by Sir J. Lubbock. Yet many of the customs he refers to, such as Bride-catching, although they may have arisen in very early times, cannot possibly have been Primeval in the strict sense of that term.

His assertion, repeated over and over again, is that mere savages "never did and never could raise themselves, unaided, into a higher condition." Now it may be perfectly true that Man never could "unaided" discover religious truth, or rise to any adequate idea of the nature, or of the demands, of moral obligation; and yet it may be wholly untrue that he is equally incompetent to discover the physical laws of nature, or to find out by mechanical skill how to adapt them to his own use. Again, Whately admits, that "when men have once reached a certain stage in the advance towards civilization, it is then possible for them (under favourable circumstances) to advance further and further in the same direction." But there is no attempt to define either what civilization in this sense means, or to specify what kind and what amount of preliminary instruction is the minimum from which further advance is rendered possible. If by civilization is meant a knowledge of the industrial arts, the doctrine that Man never did and never could "unaided" raise himself from one step in mechanical invention to another, is a doctrine involving two separate assertions which require to be separately examined. Of these two assertions, the first, that Savages never have "raised themselves," is an assertion which, from its very nature, it is difficult if not impossible to prove. Whately defies the supporter of Development to produce a single case where this has been actually done. Sir

J. Lubbock replies by defying his opponent to show that it has not been done and done often. He urges, and urges as it seems to me with truth, that the great difficulty of teaching many savages the arts of civilized life, is no proof whatever that the various degrees of advance towards the knowledge of those arts which are actually found among semi-barbarous nations, may not have been of strictly indigenous growth. Thus it appears that one tribe of Red Indians, called "Mandans," practised the art of fortifying their towns. Surrounding tribes, although they saw the advantages derived from this art, yet never practised it, and never learned it. Whately, fixing his eyes on the ruder tribes, says, "See how clear it is that savages are utterly unteachable." His opponents, fixing their eyes on the more advanced tribes, say, "See how clear it is that men once savage can invent and practise useful arts." Whately says, "Prove to me, first, that these Mandans had ever been as savage as their neighbours; and secondly, that they had raised themselves." Sir J. Lubbock replies that on the conditions laid down by Whately no such proof is possible. If any record could be found of the former condition of the Mandans, the very existence of such a record would prove former contact with civilized peoples, and if such contact were proved, Whately would attribute to such contact the improvement which is observed. On the other hand, if the Mandans had "raised themselves" from a more savage condition, without any teaching from more civilized races, there could be no record of the fact. The same objection applies to the demand made by Whately as regards all other races among whom different mechanical arts have been found established. It is impossible by counter assertions to settle dogmatically the origin of such arts, and the absence of recorded cases of indigenous advance is itself rather favourable than adverse to the theory of those who assert that such advance is possible, and has actually taken place. It is precisely when this advance has been most strictly indigenous that the preservation of the fact by record would become impossible.

I do not agree, therefore, with the late Archbishop of Dublin, that we are entitled to assume it as a fact that, as regards the mechanical arts, no savage race has ever raised itself. The other assertion that no such race ever could so raise itself, is confessedly a theory, and a theory the truth of which is by no means self-evident. In the first place, when the possibility of progress is admitted, provided some elementary instruction is supposed as a foundation on which to work, it is evident that we are dealing with a proposition altogether hazy, unless there be some clear definition of the nature and amount of this elementary instruction which is demanded. Whately says that "the earliest generations of mankind had received only very limited, and what may be called elementary instruction, enough merely to enable them to make further advances afterwards by the exercise of their natural powers." But how much was this "enough?" And what is meant by "instruction," as distinguished from inborn or intuitive powers of observation and of reasoning? May not this have been the form in which the Creator first "instructed" Man? For here it is important to observe that in direct proportion as we assume Man's Primitive Condition to have been such as to require elementary teaching, in the same proportion do we suppose that his primitive condition in respect to intellect was low and weak. Accordingly, Whately assumes as an indisputable fact, that Man has no instincts such as enable the lower animals to construct nests, and cells, and lairs. My own belief is, that this is an assumption which is not only unproved, but one which in all probability is false. As Whately himself admits, "Man is an animal" as well as the creatures that are below him. It is true that he has not instincts of the same kind as they have. But this is no proof whatever that he has not, and had not originally, instincts which stand in strict correlation with the peculiarities of his higher physical organization. This is a department of inquiry which has been far too much neglected both by physiologists and by metaphysicians. There are many facts which go far to prove that Man has, and must always have had, instincts which afford all that is required as a starting-ground for advance in the mechanical arts. Few persons have reflected on how much is involved in the most purely instinctive acts, such as the throwing of a stone, or the wielding of a stick as a weapon of offence. Both these simple acts involve the great principle of the use of artificial tools. Even in the most rudimentary form, the use of an implement fashioned for a special purpose is absolutely peculiar to Man, and arises necessarily and instinctively out of the structure of his body. The bodies of the lower animals are so constructed that such implements as they are capable of directing are all supplied in the form of bodily organs. All effects which they desire to produce, or are capable of producing, are effected directly by the use of those organs under the guidance of implanted instincts. There are some very curious cases among the lower animals of a near approach to the principle involved in the use of tools—that is to say, the use of natural force through artificial means. Thus the common Grey or Hooded Crow is constantly in the habit of lifting shell-fish to a certain height in the air, and then letting them fall upon the rocks of the shore, in order to break the shells. Some species of Monkey will even use any stone which may be at hand for the purpose of striking and breaking a nut. The Elephant tears branches from the trees and uses them as an artificial tail to fan himself and to keep off the flies. But between these rudiments of intellectual perception and the next step — that of adapting and fashioning an instrument for a particular purpose,—there is a gulf in which lies the whole immeasurable distance between Man and the brutes. In no case whatever do they ever use an implement made by themselves as an intermediate agency between their bodily organs and the work which they desire to do. Man, on the contrary, is so constructed that in almost everything he desires to do he must employ an agency intermediate between his bodily organs and the effect which he wishes to produce. But this necessity, which in one aspect is a physical disability, is correlated with a mind capable of Invention, and with certain implanted instincts which involve all the rudiments of mechanical skill. The man who first lifted a stone and threw it, practised an art which not one of the lower animals is capable of practising. This is an act which in all probability is as strictly instinctive and natural to Man as it is to a Dog to bite, or to a Bull to charge. Yet the act involves the idea and the knowledge of projectile force, and of the arts by which direction can be given to that force. The wielding of a stick is, in all probability, an act equally of primitive intuition, and from this to the throwing of a stick, and the use of javelins, is an easy and natural transition. Simple as these acts are, they involve both physical and mental powers capable of all the developments which we see in the most advanced industrial arts. These acts involve the instinctive idea of the constancy of natural causes, and the capacity of thought which gives men the conviction that what has happened under given conditions will under the same conditions always happen again. Did Dr. Whately mean that Man must have been instructed by God how to throw a stone, or to wield a stick, or to hurl a javelin, or to build a hut? And if so, at what point did such lessons in mechanics stop? Is it not evident that the more perfect we suppose the first man to have been, so far as regards at least his powers of thought, of observation, and of reflection, the less needful is it to suppose that the few and simple arts necessary for the sustenance of his life were communicated to him in any other form than that of intuitive powers of perception and discovery?

And here it is important to observe that even if savage races be taken as the type of man's Primeval Condition, the evidence afforded by these races is all in favour of the conclusion that as regards his characteristic mental powers, Man has always been Man, and nothing less. There is quite as much ingenuity and skill in the manufacture of a knife of flint, as in the manufacture of a knife of iron. And the skill displayed by the men who used stone implements is not confined to that which is involved in the selection of mineral substances suitable for the purpose. That skill is also eminently displayed in the use made of those stone implements after they had been fashioned. The smaller implements of bone, or of horn, or of wood, which the stone knives and hatchets were employed to make, are often highly ingenious, and sometimes eminently beautiful. The truth is that high qualities of reasoning and ready faculties of observation are called forth in the inverse ratio of the acquired knowledge with which they are provided and from which they start. The great ingenuity and resource shown by many of the rudest tribes in their weapons, and the sense of beauty evinced by them in the choice and in the invention of ornamental forms, have hardly been sufficiently appreciated. It is impossible, for example, to read the description given by Sir J. Richardson of the bows and arrows of the Eskimo without being struck by the admirable skill with which their scanty resources, and their limited command of natural material, are turned to the very best account. The throwing-stick of the Australian Savage is a most ingenious application of the principle of the lever. The boomerang must have been discovered, as so many other discoveries are made among ourselves, by pure accident—by some savage throwing a crooked branch, and by his observing its curious and unexpected flight. But every one of these inventions and discoveries involves and exhibits in full operation the peculiar and characteristic gifts of the human intellect. The same gifts and the same powers start in the case of each new generation from a higher vantage-ground of inherited, and therefore of accumulated knowledge; and it is thus that, without any change in their own nature, and even without any increase in their own inherent strength, they attain gradually to higher and more complicated results. And if we are to assume with the supporters of the Savage-theory that Man has himself invented all he now knows, then the very earliest inventions of our race must have been the most wonderful of all, and the richest in the fruits they bore. The men who first discovered the use of fire, and the use of those grasses which we now know under the name of corn, were discoverers compared with whom, as regards the value of their ideas to the world, Faraday and Wheatstone are but the inventors of ingenious toys.

It may possibly be true, as Whately argues, that Man never could have discovered these things without divine instruction. If so, it is fatal to the Savage-theory. But it is equally fatal to that Theory if we assume the opposite position, and suppose that the noblest discoveries ever made by Man were made by him in primeval times.

On these, as well as on other grounds, I have never attached much importance to Whately's argument. I do not mean to say that the conclusion to which it points may not possibly be true, but it is a conclusion which I look upon as incapable of positive proof.

The question of Man's Primitive Condition must therefore be approached from another side. We can only hope to reach the Unknown by reasoning from the Known; and, starting from this ground, we have the indisputable fact that Man is capable of Degradation. This is a subject which, as it appears to me, Sir J. Lubbock deals with in the most cursory and superficial manner. In fact, as far as it is possible to do so, he avoids it altogether. In his work on "Prehistoric Man" a single page exhausts all he has to say on one of the most prominent facts of History and of Nature, and this page is headed, "No Evidence of Degradation." Yet nothing in the Natural History of Man can be more certain than that both morally, and intellectually, and physically he can, and he often does, sink from a higher to a lower level. This is true of Man both collectively and individually—of men and of societies of men. Some regions of the world are strewn with the monuments of civilizations which have passed away. Rude and barbarous tribes stare with wonder on the remains of Temples, of which they cannot conceive the purpose, and of Cities which are the dens of beasts. It is not necessary to assume, as it has sometimes been assumed, that there is a law of decay affecting communities as certain in its operation as the law which operates on the individual frame. It is enough to note the indisputable fact that men are liable to degradation and decline,—and this even as regards the knowledge and the practice of those industrial arts on which the very existence of large populations may depend. As regards moral character the possibility and the fact of degradation is not less certain. It is a result only too common and familiar, both as regards individuals and societies of men. In truth this kind of decline almost always precedes the other. The higher elements of civilization depend on qualities of the mind. It is by moral and intellectual force that all the triumphs of civilization are achieved. When that force declines, the agencies of degradation establish their ascendency, and the completeness with which they have done their work is one of the standing wonders of the world. No doubt, the ancient civilizations which have been so utterly destroyed were in many cases brought to a violent, and as it may be argued, to an accidental end. They were overrun and swept away by the rush of barbarous hordes. But these are accidents which did not happen to civilized nations so long as their civilization was yet undecayed. I am far, however, from denying the powerful influence of external conditions in favouring the development of the peaceful arts, or, on the contrary, in arresting that development, or even in destroying it when it had been long established. Nor am I disposed to keep in the background the effects produced on ancient civilizations by the wars and the great primeval migrations of our race. On the contrary, these are facts which form the next step in the argument I am now maintaining —a step which goes far to connect the possibility of degradation with the known causes which have operated, and in the very nature of things must have operated, in producing it.

For it matters not which of the two theories we adopt in regard to the Origin of the Human Race, whether we suppose it to have proceeded from one or from two, or even from several different centres of creation; it matters not whether we suppose with Sir J. Lubbock that the "first being worthy to be called a Man" was born of some inferior creature, or whether we believe with Whately, that he was truly human in his powers, but required some "elementary instruction to enable his faculties to begin their work." In any case we may safely assume that Man must have begun his course in some one or more of those portions of the earth which are genial in climate, rich in natural fruits, and capable of yielding the most abundant return to the very simplest arts. It is under such conditions that the first establishment of the human race can be most easily understood; nay, it is under such conditions only that it is conceivable at all. And as these are the conditions which would favour the first establishment, and the most rapid increase of Man, so also are these the conditions under which knowledge would most rapidly accumulate, and the earliest possibilities of material civilization would arise.

Now what are the changes of external circumstance which first, in the natural course of things, would bring an adverse influence to bear upon Mankind? Here again we are on firm ground, because we know one great cause which has been always operating, and we know its natural and inevitable effects. This cause is simply the law of increase. It is the consequence of that law that population is always pressing upon the limits of subsistence. Hence the necessity of migrations, and the force which has propelled successive generations of men farther and farther. in ever-widening circles round the original centre or centres of their birth. Then, as it would always be the weaker tribes who would be driven from the ground which had become overstocked, and as the lands to which they went forth were less and less hospitable in climate and productions, the struggle for life would be always harder. And so it always happens in the natural and necessary course of things, that the races which were driven farthest would be the rudest — the most engrossed in the pursuits of mere animal existence.

And now, does not this key of principle fit into and explain all the facts? Do they not seem in the light of that explanation to take form and order? Is it not true that the lowest and rudest tribes in the population of the globe have been found at the farthest extremities of its great Continents, and in the distant Islands which would be the last refuge of the victims of violence and misfortune? "The New World" is the Continent which presents the most uninterrupted stretch of habitable land from the highest northern to the lowest southern latitude. On the extreme north we have the Eskimo,* or Inuit race, maintaining human life under conditions of extremest hardship, even amid the perpetual ice of the Polar Seas. And what a life it is! Watching at the blow-hole of a seal for many hours, in a temperature of 75° below freezing point, is the constant work of the

* I have adopted the form of this name (usually spelt Esquimaux), which is adopted as the most correct by Sir J. Richardson in his work on the Polar Seas. "Inuit" is the native Eskimo name for their own race.

Inuit hunter.* And when at last his prey is struck, it is his luxury to feast upon the raw blood and blubber. To civilized Man it is hardly possible to conceive a life so wretched, and in many respects so brutal as the life led by this race during the long lasting night of the arctic winter. Not even the most extravagant theorist as regards the plurality of Human Origins, can suppose that there was an Eskimo Adam—that any man was originally created or developed in the icy regions round the Pole. Here then we have a case beyond all question, of races driven by wars and migrations, from

* Very curious details on Eskimo hunting, feasting, and habits generally are given in Captain C. F. Hall's most interesting work, "Life with the Esquimaux." (Sampson Low, Son, & Marston. 1864.)

the more temperate regions of the globe. So long as they were still in those regions, the ancestors of the Eskimo must have lived in another manner, and must have had wholly different habits. They may have practised such simple agriculture as we know was practised among the most ancient people who have left their remains in the Swiss Lake Dwellings. They may have been nomads living on their flocks and herds. But neither an agricultural nor a pastoral life is possible on the borders of a frozen sea. The rigours of the region they now inhabit have reduced this people to the condition in which we now see them, and whatever arts their fathers knew, suited to more genial climates, have been, and could not fail to be, utterly forgotten. It is a very remarkable fact that this process, by which even the most sterile regions of the globe have been peopled, is a process which appears to be still in operation. Arctic voyagers have long known that there are lands nearer the Pole than those which they have hitherto been able to reach, and it has been even suspected that there exists there a somewhat milder climate and a more open sea. A whaling ship, which in 1867 reached a more northern point than had hitherto been attained, has brought the curious information that a tribe wandering near Cape Chelagskoi had recently driven another tribe before them across the Frozen Sea to a land lying so far north that only its mountain tops could be occasionally seen from the Siberian Headlands.* This farther land has never yet been trodden by civilized Man; and if he ever does reach it, he will thus probably find it occupied by men who may have forgotten how and whence their fathers came.

And now let us pass to the other extremity of the great Continent of America—to Cape Horn, and to the Island off it, which projects its desolate rocks into one of the most inhospitable climates in the world. The inhabitants of Tierra del Fuego are perhaps the most degraded among the races of mankind. How could they be otherwise? "Their country," says Mr. Darwin, "is a broken

* See letter in the *Times* of December 30, 1867, from Captain Sherard Osborne.

mass of wild rocks, lofty hills, and useless forests; and these are viewed through mists and endless storms. The habitable land is reduced to the stones of the beach. In search of food they are compelled to wander unceasingly from spot to spot, and so steep is the coast that they can only move about in their wretched canoes." They are habitual cannibals, killing and eating their old women before they kill their dogs, for the sufficient reason, as explained by themselves—"Doggies catch otters, old women no." Of some of these people who came round the *Beagle* in their canoes, the same author says—"These were the most wretched and miserable creatures I anywhere beheld. They were quite naked, and even one full-grown woman was absolutely so. It was raining heavily, and the fresh water, together with the spray, trickled down her body. In another harbour not far distant, a woman, who was suckling a new-born child, came one day alongside the vessel and remained there out of mere curiosity, whilst the sleet fell and thawed on her naked bosom and on the skin of her naked baby. These poor wretches were stunted in their growth, their hideous faces bedaubed with white paint, their skins filthy and greasy, their hair entangled, their voices discordant, and their gestures violent. Viewing such men, one can hardly make oneself believe that they are fellow-creatures and inhabitants of the same world." Well might Darwin add, "Whilst beholding these savages one asks, Whence have they come? What could have tempted, or what change compelled, a tribe of men to leave the fine regions of the North, to travel down the Cordillera, or backbone of America, to invent and build canoes which are not used by the tribes of Chili, Peru, and Brazil, and then to enter on one of the most inhospitable countries within the limits of the globe?" * There can be but one explanation. Quarrels and wars between tribe and tribe, induced by the mere increase of numbers and the consequent pressure on the means of subsistence, have been always, ever since Man existed, driving the weaker races farther and farther from the older settlements of mankind. And when the ultimate points of the

* Darwin's "Naturalist's Voyage," ed. 1852, p. 216.

habitable world are reached, the conditions of existence cause and necessitate a savage and degraded life. Darwin gives the true explanation of their condition when he says, "How little can the higher powers of the mind be brought into play! What is there for imagination to picture, for reason to compare, for judgment to decide upon?" The case of the Fuegians is a case in which there can be no doubt whatever of the causes of their degraded condition. On every side of them, and in proportion as we recede from their wretched country, the surrounding tribes are less wretched and better acquainted with the simpler arts. And it is remarkable that in the case of this people we have proof of another point of great interest and importance, viz., this—that even the most degraded savages have all the perfect attributes of humanity, which can be and are developed, the moment they are placed under favourable conditions. Captain Fitzroy had in 1830 carried off some of these people to England, where they were taught the habits and the arts of civilized life. Of one of these who was taken back to his own country in the *Beagle*, Mr. Darwin tells us that his "intellect was good," and of another that he had a "nice disposition." We see, therefore, that every fact and circumstance connected with the Fuegians agrees with the supposition that their "utter barbarism" was due entirely to the cruel conditions of their life, and the wretched country into which they had been driven. The Bushmen of South Africa are another case in point. It seems to be clearly ascertained that they belong to the same race as other tribes who are far less degraded, and that they are simply the descendants of outcasts driven to the woods and rocks.* So, again, among the great islands of the Pacific, the natives of Van Diemen's Land were the most utterly degraded of all the Polynesian races.

With these facts staring us in the face, connecting themselves in an obvious order with causes which we know to be all operating in one direction, is it not absurd to argue that the condition of these outcasts of the human family can be assumed as

* Pritchard's "Natural History of Man," vol. ii.

representing the aboriginal condition of Man? Is it not certain that whatever advances towards civilization may have been made among their progenitors, such advances must necessarily have been lost under the conditions to which their children are reduced? Sir J. Lubbock urges, in reply to Whately, that the low condition of Australian savages affords no proof whatever that they could not raise themselves, because the materials of improvement are wanting in that country, which affords no cereals, nor animals capable of useful domestication. But Sir J. Lubbock does not perceive that the same argument which shows how improvement could not possibly be attained, shows also how degradation could not possibly be avoided. If with the few resources of the country it was impossible for savages to rise, it follows that with those same resources it would be impossible for a half-civilized race not to fall. And as in this case again, unless we are to suppose a separate Adam and Eve for Van Diemen's Land, its natives must originally have come from one or other of the great continents where both corn and cattle were to be had, it follows that the low condition of these natives is much more likely to have been the result of degradation than of primeval barbarism. Man as an animal does not belong to the Fauna of Australia. The scientific evidence, therefore, is conclusive that he came to it from other lands. But it is highly improbable that the circumstances of his arrival in the Islands were such as would have enabled him to bring either corn or cattle with him. Whatever knowledge of these things he had before, must necessarily have been lost. The present condition, therefore, of the Australian Savage in respect to these important elements of civilization, affords no presumption whatever that it represents the condition of those from whom he is descended. There is hardly a single fact quoted by Sir J. Lubbock in favour of his own theory, which, when viewed in connection with the same indisputable principles, does not tell against that theory rather than in its favour. The facts indeed which I have hitherto quoted prove only that forgetfulness of arts once practised and of knowledge once possessed, must inevitably have arisen among tribes driven into inhospitable regions. But there are other facts also referred to by Sir J. Lubbock himself, which show that there are cases in which we have proof of this process having actually taken place. Thus, in regard to the Eskimo, he quotes the case of a tribe in Baffin's Bay who "could not be made to understand what was meant by war, nor had they any warlike weapons."* No wonder, poor people! They had been driven into regions where no stronger race could desire to follow them. But that their fathers had once known what war and violence meant, there is no more conclusive

* "Prehistoric Times," p. 410.

proof than the dwelling-place of their children. So again, Sir J. Lubbock quotes the testimony of Cook in respect to the Tasmanians, that they had no canoes. Yet their ancestors could not have reached the island by walking on the sea. Some of the tribes did not know how fire could be obtained if it were once extinguished.* Again, of the Australians, Sir J. Lubbock reminds us that in a cave on the north-west coast "tolerable figures of sharks, porpoises, turtles, lizards, canoes, and some quadrupeds," &c., were found; and yet that the present natives of the country where they were found were utterly incapable of realizing the most vivid artistic representations, and ascribed the draw-

* "Prehistoric Times," pp. 354-5.

ings in the cave to diabolical agency.* In all these cases we have direct evidences of degradation or of forgetfulness, even since Man first reached the shores of those distant Islands, and we see how it could not fail to be so under the known effect of known cause upon the condition of our race.

And now we can better estimate the value to be set on the arguments which have been founded on the rude implements found in the river drifts and in the caves of northern Europe. I, for one, accept the evidence which Geology affords that these implements are of very ancient date. I accept too the evidence which that science affords, that these implements were in all probability the ice

* "Prehistoric Times," p. 348.

hatchets and rude knives used by tribes which towards the close of the Glacial Age had pushed their way to the farthest limits of the lands which were then habitable. And what follows? The inevitable conclusion is, that it must be about as safe to argue from those implements as to the condition of Man at that time in the countries of his Primeval Home, as it would be in our own day to argue from the habits and arts of the Eskimo as to the state of civilization in London or in Paris.

For here I must observe that Archæologists are using language on this subject which, if not positively erroneous, requires, at least, more rigorous definitions and limitations of meaning than they are disposed to attend to They talk of an Old Stone Age (Palæolithic), and of a Newer Stone Age (Neolithic) and of a Bronze Age, and of an Iron Age. Now, there is no proof whatever that such Ages ever existed in the world. It may be true, and it probably is true, that all nations in the progress of the Arts have passed through the stages of using stone for implements before they were acquainted with the use of metals. But knowledge of the metals must have arisen at very different epochs in different regions of the earth. In South Africa flint implements have lately been discovered in abundance, but over a large portion of that vast continent the knowledge and the use of iron seems to have been of very ancient date; and I am informed by Sir Samuel Baker that iron ore is so common in Africa, and of a kind so easily reducible by heat, that its use might well be discovered by the rudest tribes. As a matter of fact, they are now all excellent workers in iron. Then again, it is to be remembered that there are some countries in the world where stone is as rare and difficult to get as metals. In them the use of stone implements may imply even an extended commerce. The great alluvial plains of Mesopotamia are a case in point. Accordingly, we know from the remains of the First Chaldæan Monarchy that a very high civilization in the arts of agriculture and of commerce co-existed with the use of stone implements of a very rude character.* This

* Rawlinson's "Five Great Monarchies," vol. i. pp. 119, 120.

fact proves that rude stone implements are not necessarily any indication whatever of a really barbarous condition. Assuming then that the use of stone has in all cases preceded the use of metals, it is quite certain that the same Age which was an Age of Stone in one part of the world was an Age of Metal in another. As regards the Eskimo and the South-Sea Islanders we are now, or were very recently, living in a Stone Age. And so it has been in all past times of which any record remains. The whole argument therefore which has been founded on flint implements, is an argument liable to these two fundamental objections, first that flint implements are a very uncertain index of civilization, even among the tribes who used them; and secondly that they are no index at all of the state of civilization among other tribes who lived at the same time in other portions of the globe. The finding of flint implements for example, however rude, in England, or in Denmark, or in France, affords no evidence whatever of the condition of the Industrial Arts in the same age upon the banks of the Euphrates or the Nile.

There is one argument of Sir J. Lubbock in favour of the Savage-theory, which I observe with as much astonishment as that which he expresses in reference to some of the arguments of Whately. Sir J. Lubbock says that some savages have been found who have no religion at all. Such, he argues, was probably the condition of Primeval Man, because he "feels it difficult to believe that any people which once possessed a religion would ever entirely lose it." Surely, if there is one fact more certain than another in respect to the nature of Man, it is that he is capable of losing religious knowledge, of ceasing to believe in religious truth, and of falling away from religious duty. If by "religion" is meant the existence merely of some impressions of powers invisible and "supernatural"—even this, we know, can not only be lost, but be scornfully disavowed by men who are highly civilized. Nor does Sir J. Lubbock's comment upon this subject gain by the further explanation which he gives. He says that "Religion appeals so strongly to the hopes and fears of men, it takes so deep a hold on most minds, it is so great a consolation in times of sorrow and sickness, that I can hardly think any nation would ever abandon it altogether." There are two obvious replies to such reasoning: the first is, that many false religions do not answer to this description so far as regards their self-recommending and consoling power; the second is, that neither does true religion answer this description to those who are corrupt and vicious. Belief in a God who is "of purer eyes than to behold iniquity" is a belief which bad men may not have liked to cherish. As regards the first of these two replies, Sir J. Lubbock himself bears emphatic testimony to its force. In his work on "Prehistoric Man," speaking of the savage, he says,* "Thus his life is one prolonged scene of selfishness and fear; even in his religion, if he has any, *he creates for himself a new source of terror, and peoples the world with invisible enemies.*" Yes, and this is mildly stated. The most cruel and savage customs in the world are the direct effect of its "religions." And if men could drop religions when they would, or if they could even form the wish to get rid of those which sit like a nightmare on their life, there would be many more nations without a "religion" than there are found to be. But religions can neither be put on nor cast off like garments, according to their utility, or ac-

* P. 484.

cording to their beauty, or according to their power of comforting. Among the causes which have determined their form and character in different nations we must reckon the moral corruption of human nature. I am not speaking of this corruption in a dogmatic and theological sense; I speak of it as an unquestionable fact, whatever be the history of its origin. By the corruption of human nature, I mean the undeniable fact that Man has a constant tendency to abuse his powers, to do what according even to his own standard of right or wrong he knows he ought not to do; to be unjust and cruel towards others, and to fall into horrible and degrading superstitions. Human corruption in this sense is as much a fact in the natural history of Man as that he is a Biped without feathers. It is entirely independent of any belief, or any theory as to Man's original condition. Sir J. Lubbock's argument implies that the tribes, if such there be, (which, by the way, is extremely doubtful) who are not known to have any ideas at all in respect to spiritual beings or to another world, are in a lower condition than tribes which have a "religion," however cruel and horrible its rites may be. According to this theory, even devil-worship would be a step in ascent towards "civilization" from the "utter barbarism" of Primeval Man. But this is a theory as contrary to reason as it is contrary to all the evidence we have on the history of Man. The farther we go back in that history the more clear become the traces of some pure traditions, and the rays of some primeval light. Such evidence as history and philosophy and criticism afford on the course of religious knowledge is not in favour of the doctrine of a gradual rise, but, on the contrary, of continuous corruption and decline. "If there is one thing," says Professor Max Müller, "which a comparative study of religions places in the clearest light, it is the inevitable decay to which every religion is exposed . . . . Whenever we can trace back a religion to its first beginnings, we find it free from many blemishes that affected it in its later stages."* One of the most ancient religions of the world is re-

* "Chips from a German Workshop," vol. i., pref., xxiii.

presented in its earlier form in the Sanskrit Vedas, and the contrast between its doctrines and those of existing Hindooism is but a sample of the working of a great law which can be traced in every region of the world. This is no case confined to some little corner of the earth, or to some short period of time, or to some partial and accidental cause. It is the case of a religion which in all its branches embraces uncounted millions of the human race, and the history of which extends over more than 3,000 years. Nor is the sense in which corruption and decay are predicated of this religion at all vague or indefinite. It has become lower, ruder, more corrupt,—in its conceptions of the Divine Nature,—in its notions of acceptable worship, and in the social institutions which are connected with Belief.

The truth is, that Man's capacities of degradation stand in close relation, and are proportionate, to his capacities of improvement. What faculty of the human mind lies nearer to the very centre of its highest life than the faculty of Imagination? Without it we could not interpret Nature, or form any conception of its laws, or feel their harmony, or understand their use. Without it we could not see the Abstract or read the Future. Without it we should be without motive to resist Impulse, or to maintain Conviction, or to rise to Duty. We could form no idea whatever of Religion. It would not be possible to desire the Unknown or to hope for the

Unseen. And yet Pascal was not wrong when he placed this same faculty of Imagination at the very head of the "Deceitful Powers." For it is, in truth, one of the most effective causes and instruments of Degradation. It is its function to give form and expression to all those vague emotions which arise inevitably out of contact between the mind that is in Man and the mind that is in Nature. These emotions are literally what the Poet calls them—"the blank misgivings of a creature moving about in worlds not realized." But without Knowledge given or acquired, to guide the elements in Imagination which are purely intellectual, and without virtue to control the elements which are chiefly moral, this "Superb Power," as Pascal also most justly calls it, does terrible work indeed. It is the mother and the nurse of all the horrible inventions of Idolatry. Through its operation have arisen, from time to time, all the diabolical rites which have degraded, and do still degrade, so many tribes of men far below the level of the brutes. But irrational as the superstitions of heathen nations may appear to be, and even inconceivable in a Being who is capable of reason, it should never be forgotten that this is true only of the last developments of Idolatry, and is by no means true of its first beginnings. On the contrary, these are among the most natural of all spiritual temptations, and perhaps the most difficult to resist. The first of the Commandments is of all others the most difficult to obey: "Thou shalt have no other Gods before Me." The dependence of the human mind on outward symbols, and then its tendency to identify the symbols with the conceptions they represent—these are the roots of all Idolatry. The course of thought, in our own day, even among highly civilized and enlightened men, may well remind us how easy and how natural it is to lapse into systems of belief, which in their fundamental character are essentially Creature-worship. The fact is, that so far from there being any difficulty in understanding how spiritual truth, once known, could be ever lost, all observation and experience prove that it is the most difficult of all things to maintain with even tolerable purity any high standard of spiritual faith. A thousand tendencies from within, and from without, are perpetually at work to undermine, or to transform it. And then the awful correlations of Human Thought render it not only probable but inevitable that the first departures from the knowledge and the love of Truth, must end in wider and wider divergence from it. The infinite subtlety and ingenuity of Imagination will, when it is ignorant and corrupt amply account for the origin and growth of even the most degraded superstitions. This is a subject too extensive to be pursued here; but it could be shown that even among the South Sea Islanders, and other tribes who have been driven farthest from the original settlements of Man, there were many religious customs of which those who practised them did not know the origin or the meaning, and which clearly indicated their derivation from an older, a more intelligible, but a forgotten faith.

This is also eminently true of the religious rites and practices of some of the Hill tribes of India. A most curious and interesting account of human sacrifices by the Khonds, one of the Hill Tribes of Orissa, has been published by my friend, Major-General John Campbell, who has been mainly instrumental, under the Government of India, in the abolition of this horrid rite. The absolute rule that the victims must be procured by purchase, stands in unmistakeable relation to the only intelligible principle in the very idea of sacrifice, namely, the principle of self-sacrifice.

Here for the present I must leave the subject. My chief object has been to show how little really depends on some of the arguments which have been put forth by both sides in this controversy, and to indicate what seems to me to be the true bearing of the facts which as yet have been clearly ascertained. I set little value on the argument of Whately, that as regards the mechanical arts Man can never have risen "unaided." The aid which Man had from his Creator may possibly have been nothing more than the aid of a Body and of a Mind, so marvellously endowed, that Thought was an instinct, and Contrivance was at once a necessity and a delight. But I set still less value on the arguments of Sir J. Lubbock, that Primeval Man must have been born in a state of "utter barbarism," on the ground that this is the actual condition of the outcasts of our race, or that industrial knowledge has advanced from small beginnings, or that there are traces of rude customs among many nations now highly civilized. None of these arguments afford any proof whatever, or even any reasonable presumption, in favour of the conclusion which they are employed to support: first, because along with a complete ignorance of the Arts it is quite possible that there may have been a higher knowledge of God, and a closer communion with Him; secondly, because many cases of existing barbarism can be distinctly traced to adverse external circumstances, and because it is at least possible that all real barbarism has had its origin in like conditions; thirdly, because the known character of Man and the indisputable facts of history prove that he has within him at all times the elements of corruption—that even in his most civilized condition, he is capable of degradation, that his Knowledge may decay, and that his Religion may be lost.

www.ingramcontent.com/pod-product-compliance
Lightning Source LLC
LaVergne TN
LVHW011209110826
845150LV00006B/1382
9781425517854